D1369610

spdri srlhn
dcly + TSi
sdn TS*

Joe M. Pullis, Ed.D.

**Professor, Department of Office Administration
and Business Communication
College of Administration and Business
Louisiana Tech University**

GLENCOE/McGRAW-HILL
A Macmillan/McGraw-Hill Company
Mission Hills, California

***Speedwriting* SHORTHAND DICTATION
AND TRANSCRIPTION STUDENT TRANSCRIPT**

Copyright © 1987 by Glencoe Publishing Company, a division of Macmillan, Inc.
Copyright © 1984, 1977 by The Bobbs-Merrill Company, Inc.
Copyright © 1975, 1973, 1966, 1965, 1964, 1954, 1951, 1950, 1925 by Speedwriting
Publishing Company, Inc.

Send all inquiries to:
Glencoe/McGraw-Hill
15319 Chatsworth Street
P.O. Box 9609
Mission Hills, CA 91346-9609

ISBN 0-02-685140-7

3 4 5 6 7 8 9   95 94 93 92 91 90

LESSON

1

1

Dear Mrs. Rogers:

Recently I completed my courses in business education and am now looking forward[1] to a career in office work. I wish to tell you that I especially enjoyed your courses in typing[2] and shorthand, and I learned much from the classes you taught.

Because most of my office training has occurred under your[3] direction, a recommendation from you would be very helpful in finding my first job. May I please list your[4] name as a reference on my resumé?

I have appreciated your guidance over the last two years, and[5] I feel that I am well prepared to accept a position as secretary. I will do my best to justify[6] the interest you have shown in me. Sincerely, (129)

2

Dear Mrs. Rogers:

We are considering one of your students, Jennifer West, for the position of correspondence[1] secretary. She received a high rating on both the shorthand and the typing tests, and she also made[2] a favorable impression during her interview.

The person we hire must produce a large volume of[3] correspondence daily. In a few cases, this person will also be responsible for writing answers to[4] routine letters of inquiry.

Therefore, we are looking for a person who is dependable, uses good judgment,[5] and shows a willingness to assume responsibility. Would you recommend Jennifer for a position[6] requiring these qualities?

We would appreciate receiving your reply within one week in order to make[7] our decision. Very truly yours, (146)

3

Dear Mr. Watson:

Thank you for your letter of application. We have always encouraged the placement office[1] of your college to refer good students to us. As a result, we have many fine employees from your school.

As[2] part of our current expansion, we will soon open a new store downtown. At that time we will move our central[3] offices to that location. We have plans to increase personnel in several departments. Because of your[4] extensive background in data processing and accounting, you might qualify for some of the new positions[5] we are developing. The work experience described in your letter might also be appropriate for our[6] credit department.

I suggest that we discuss these opportunities in person. If you would call my office[7] for an appointment, I could arrange to meet with you one day next week. Yours very truly, (155)

4

Dear Ms. White:

Part of the reward of being a teacher is watching young and eager minds develop in my classroom.[1] When an exceptional student comes along, it is especially rewarding to see that person receive[2] a challenging job. This year it gives me particular pleasure to recommend someone who has worked hard and learned[3] quickly since beginning his study here.

Jerry Fields has taken great care to prepare himself for a successful[4] career in business offices. When he is working on a project, he gives full attention to details, organizes[5] his work well, and uses his time efficiently. He works well independently and submits completed[6] assignments on time.

Jerry is quiet, gets along well with other people, and behaves in a professional[7] manner. I am convinced that you would be pleased with his performance. Cordially yours, (154)

5

Dear Barbara:

Now that I have had the opportunity to study your employment papers at length, I do[1] have some suggestions.

Employers look for a person who has work experience or an impressive academic[2] record. They also look for dependability, basic office skills, and a desire to succeed on the[3] job.

Use your resumé to accomplish all of the things listed above. Demonstrate organizational skills[4] by listing information in a logical order. Demonstrate typing and spelling skills by presenting a[5] final copy that is attractive and free of errors.

Remember that you are well trained for the position you[6] are seeking. If you improve the image of your product, you will have a document that speaks highly of your[7] qualifications. Yours truly, (145)

LESSON

2

1

Dear Ray:

I received the attached letter of application from a young college student. Be-

cause it is unusual,[1] I am bringing it to your attention. If you can't suggest a position for him, perhaps you could send[2] copies of the letter to our other stores.

The young man appears to be creative, intelligent, and eager[3] to make a good impression. He has used his letter to demonstrate his ability to sell products. In this[4] case, the product is himself.

His knowledge of our equipment might be useful in other ways. For example, do[5] we have an opening in our advertising department? Public relations would be another possibility,[6] and we frequently need additional help in preparing our sales catalog.

Qualified people are[7] difficult to find. I would not want to overlook this one. Sincerely, (153)

2

Dear Mr. Jordan:

When I met my first computer, I knew this was no ordinary relationship. As soon[1] as I learned to speak its language, I was past the point of no return. I fell in love with modern automation.[2]

I wish to spend my life in the company of computers—all types, sizes, and price ranges. My greatest hope is[3] to pass my appreciation on to customers who are looking for guidance in buying and operating[4] their own equipment.

Mr. Jordan, I hope you will consider me for a sales position in your store. My[5] knowledge is extensive and current. I am a member of two computer clubs, and I subscribe to the leading[6] magazines.

Please let me know if you can use my abilities. Very truly yours, (134)

3

Dear Miss Doyle:

I am pleased to recommend to your firm

a person who has been an outstanding employee in our[1] department store. Janet Webb has worked here since graduating from college. She has been promoted to department[2] manager and was being considered for further advancement when she informed us that personal circumstances[3] would make it necessary for her to move to your city.

She has an impressive knowledge of fashion, and[4] our customers have learned to trust her judgment. In addition to her regular duties, she has organized training[5] sessions for new employees and helped plan several sales promotions.

I believe that Janet is a capable[6] person for the position you described and will contribute greatly to the success of your retail business.[7] Please let me know if I can be of further assistance. Sincerely yours, (153)

4

Dear Mr. Dobson:

We are delighted that you have joined our firm and will be moving your family to Boston[1] next month. Please allow us to help in any way we can.

As we discussed earlier, our company will assume[2] complete responsibility for your move. We have a contract with a local moving firm which provides all[3] transportation services for new employees. This company has an excellent record and can be trusted to[4] handle your finest items.

I am enclosing a brochure from the moving agent. This information will[5] answer many of your questions and help you plan your move. As soon as you have decided on an approximate date[6] for your move, please phone our office to make specific plans.

Because we know that relocating can be difficult,[7] we will do all we can to make

you feel comfortable here. Yours truly, (153)

5

Dear Mr. Moore:

This letter is to confirm your appointment for Thursday afternoon. As we discussed by telephone,[1] I received your letter and resumé. However, it is always a good idea to bring an extra[2] copy when you come for the interview.

If it is possible, we will fill this position by the middle of[3] next week. Our current supervisor is leaving at the end of the month, and we would like her replacement to have[4] the benefit of working with her.

You will meet with several people while you are here. We believe that a good[5] introduction to the facility and staff helps an applicant to understand our operations and[6] decide if he or she wishes to become an employee.

When you arrive, please register at the front desk. Someone[7] will then direct you to my office. Yours very truly, (150)

LESSON ▰▰▰▰▰▰▰▰▰▰

3

1

Dear Miss Robinson:

Thank you for your letter inquiring about possible openings in our office.

Although[1] we have no job for you at this time, we are making a special notation to contact you when something becomes[2] available. Because of your previous employment with our company, your application will be given[3] priority over others. You have worked in our claims department during the last two summers, and your supervisor[4] was very pleased with your performance.

Your more recent experience with word processing will also be[5] helpful. This is a department in which we frequently see change and expansion. We will certainly let you know[6] if an appropriate position develops.

If you have not heard from us within three months, please write again.[7] Cordially yours, (142)

2

MEMO TO: Eric Hunter

After giving much thought to the matter, I am requesting a transfer to an office[1] located in our western division.

I approach this request with mixed feelings. I have enjoyed working in[2] this community very much. However, I am under the care of a physician who feels that the weather[3] in Denver would have a positive effect on my health.

I hope the company will consider my previous[4] record in making its decision. Recent accomplishments include developing new materials for the[5] process for testing machines. I also designed a more efficient system for controlling oil flow.

I look forward[6] to my future with this company. I would now like the opportunity to make these same kinds of contributions[7] in the Denver office. (146)

3

Dear Fred:

After nine years with this company, I have made the difficult decision to resign from my duties[1] as manager of marketing and sales. National Publications has asked me to become its general[2] manager, and

this is a position I find too exciting to refuse.

In my new office I will be planning[3] and directing an expansion program which will include several new product lines. I will always be interested[4] in your firm, and I wish you continued success. I am counting on seeing many of my friends at business[5] conventions. We can all catch up on news and exchange ideas.

My departure date will be August 18.[6] Until I leave, I will do all I can to aid the transfer of responsibilities to my replacement. Yours[7] very truly, (143)

4

Dear Ms. Gregory:

We have read your letter with great interest. Your study of languages and your previous[1] work experience are most impressive. It might be possible to find a place for you immediately in[2] our international division.

Although the manager of that division is currently out of the country,[3] I could arrange a meeting with her assistant. Such a meeting would enable you to learn about our network[4] of agencies. If you then decide to apply for a specific position, I can arrange an appointment[5] with the manager during the second week of June.

Please let me know whether or not you wish to come. You may[6] reach me directly at 312-0401. Very truly yours, (133)

5

Dear Mr. Richards:

I wish to thank you again for recommending a candidate for our position of branch[1] manager. Your agency has referred excellent people to us in the past, and we look forward to continuing[2] that relationship.

We must select someone with extensive experience in management. It is equally[3] important that he or she be trained in finance. Although some legal knowledge is helpful in issuing contracts,[4] it is not necessary.

The gentleman you described yesterday has excellent qualifications, and[5] he has agreed to meet with us on February 3. We do not, however, anticipate making a[6] decision for several weeks. Because of the nature of this position, we will interview as many[7] applicants as necessary to find the most capable person. Sincerely yours, (154)

LESSON
4

1

Dear Dr. Harper:

Your acceptance of this position came as wonderful news. Your experience in electronics[1] and computer science will be of great value to us.

There are two very important projects which will[2] begin shortly after you arrive. In order to give you background information on them, I am enclosing[3] two reports for you to read now. I know that you are very busy with moving preparations, but I feel[4] certain that the time spent on these reports will prove very worthwhile when you begin your work here.

We are looking forward[5] to the contributions you will make to our program. If there is anything my office can do to assist you[6] in getting settled here, please let me know. Very truly yours, (131)

2

Dear Mary:

We are expanding our operations in data processing, and I am writing to ask you to[1] recommend a student who is skilled in accounting or bookkeeping. This person must be reliable and ready[2] to assume a full level of responsibility.

Can you suggest someone who meets these qualifications?[3] If the answer is yes, please have the eligible candidate call me as soon as possible. We have a[4] thorough training program for new employees, and we would like to enroll your student right away.

You have always[5] been an excellent resource for us, Mary. We value your judgment. I hope you can help us once again. Sincerely[6] yours, (121)

3

Dear Mrs. Miller:

Thank you for inviting me to become a member of your staff. I am pleased that you have shown[1] confidence in my ability.

When we talked last week, I did not believe that I would be able to continue[2] my college education. However, that situation suddenly changed when I was offered a full[3] scholarship. Although it means that I cannot accept your generous offer, I feel that I must take advantage[4] of this educational opportunity.

It would have been a pleasure working with you. From the description[5] you gave me, I was certain that this position was the right one for me.

If you should need extra help during the[6] summer, I would be glad to be of assistance. I will write to you again in April to see what you have[7] decided. Sincerely, (143)

4

Dear Mr. Olson:

Thank you for taking the time to meet with me this afternoon. During my interview two things[1] became immediately apparent. The working conditions in your department are very pleasant, and your[2] staff is quite supportive.

I would be eager to work for American Electronics. I would regard the job[3] as challenging and as an opportunity to increase my skills. I would also take advantage of your[4] policy of providing further education for employees.

Mr. Olson, I know that I can contribute[5] the kind of dedication you are looking for. If you have further questions about my qualifications or[6] experience, I hope you will allow me to answer them. Yours very truly, (134)

5

Dear Mr. Cox:

Thank you for your fine letter of recommendation. You will be pleased to hear that it was effective.[1] In fact, my new employer commented that he has rarely seen a more favorable recommendation.[2]

Depending upon how long it takes to make the arrangements, I will be moving to my new home very soon. I[3] anticipate many other changes ahead. My duties will be varied, and the workload will be quite demanding.[4] Needless to say, this is the opportunity I have long waited for, and I am certain that I will be[5] using all of the skills I have worked so hard to develop.

Your support has meant a great deal to me. I hope that[6] someday I will be able to help someone as you have helped me. Cordially yours, (134)

LESSON

5

1

Dear Shelley:

I now have the files for half of the people who applied for the position of administrative[1] assistant. Enclosed is a list of the remaining applicants. Could you read through their resumés before meeting[2] with me later this week?

Please select the five applicants who are most likely to meet our standards. Make your decision[3] on the basis of the skills and experience listed on their employment papers.

I will ask my secretary[4] to contact our final candidates and arrange for personal interviews. We will then write letters to[5] the references and make our final decision. I am hopeful that we will have this position filled on[6] schedule. Sincerely, (123)

2

Dear Jill:

It is good news that you have decided to relocate. We always felt that you were the best possible[1] choice to manage our regional headquarters in Tampa. One look at your performance record confirmed that you are[2] exactly what this establishment needs.

We encourage you to put your leadership skills to good use. If you wish[3] to make organizational changes, remember that the home office will support you in every way.

Until[4] you have decided upon a permanent residence, you will be the guest of this company. I think you will[5] find that your hotel is very comfortable and convenient.

This is a great opportunity. I know you[6] will make the most of it. Sincerely yours, (127)

3

Dear Employee:

Welcome to Best Industries. The enclosed materials will help introduce you to our firm. The[1] first booklet explains company policies and the layout of our facility.

An important part of your[2] benefit plan is medical and life insurance. We advise you to read this literature carefully. The[3] blue book describes your hospitalization and out-patient benefits. The red book explains the life insurance[4] policy. If you wish to increase your coverage to include other members of the family, that option[5] is presented on page 3.

After you have been employed here for six months, you will be eligible to participate[6] in our profit plan. We think our stock options are among the best in the country.

We hope this information[7] answers many of your initial questions. Yours truly, (151)

4

Dear Mr. Lee:

You were suggested to me as someone who would have information on applying for an[1] appointment overseas. I am attaching a personal data sheet describing my academic training and[2] work experience. As you can see from my record, I have studied two other languages. I would certainly[3] be willing to learn additional ones.

In addition to typing and shorthand, I have skills in office procedures[4] and word processing. Although I have always been interested in public relations and communications,[5] I would not want to limit my choices to those areas only.

I enjoy world travel and would welcome[6] the experience of living abroad. Cordially yours, (130)

5

Dear Ms. Martin:

I am pleased to accept the terms we discussed yesterday. As we agreed in our phone conversation,[1] I will begin my new duties on October 5. If it is convenient for you, I will arrive early that[2] morning to complete the paperwork you need.

I appreciate your willingness to allow me this additional[3] time. As a result, I will be able to complete many things that I had already started in my present[4] job. Once I am situated in your outstanding new facility, I will look forward to beginning[5] new research projects.

Thank you again for making me comfortable during my visit. Please tell your associates[6] that I enjoyed their pleasant introduction to the city. Very truly yours, (136)

LESSON

6

1

Dear Mr. Howard:

Our annual Christmas party is now being planned. I am writing to ask for your help in[1] making the arrangements. Last year your company provided all of the food, tables, and table settings. Your[2] employees did such a fine job that we would like them to handle the entire event again this year.

We are thinking[3] of moving the party to our company cafeteria in order to have a larger area. It[4] would be helpful if you and I could look at the space before deciding on specific arrangements. Why don't you[5] call my office to set a time for us to get together? My schedule is very flexible next week, and I[6] am certain that we can find a time that is satisfactory for both of us. Sincerely yours, (137)

2

Dear Mr. Clay:

I will be happy to set aside a day for discussing office careers with your class. Engineering[1] firms are looking for particular skills in office employees. Our work is so technical that a knowledge[2] of science is important even for beginning positions. Students who have studied science and math definitely[3] have an advantage over those who have not. When we have openings on our staff, we look for talented[4] people who are willing to continue learning.

As you know, we have employed many people from your school. They have[5] shown outstanding ability in both science and office skills. I hope you will continue to provide us[6] with such capable young men and women.

I will plan to meet you at the main entrance at 9 o'clock Friday[7] morning. Yours truly, (143)

3

Dear Mr. Michael:

We would like to sponsor several trips for our employees. Here is a very general[1] description of what we have in mind. If it can be done economically, we would like to charter a bus[2] for several trips to local areas of interest. To make the idea practical, the trips must be[3] limited to the state of Florida and must be short enough to be completed within one day. If a special[4] reduced rate is available, we would consider adding a weekend trip to Miami Beach.

I have appointed[5] a committee to make the travel arrangements. After you have given these ideas some thought, would you plan[6] to meet with this committee? We are hoping that you will have some exciting suggestions for us. Cordially yours,[7] (140)

4

MEMO TO: All Employees

Our south parking lot will be repaired and painted during the next two weeks. Although[1] we do not wish to create an inconvenience for employees, it will be necessary to limit parking during[2] this period. In order to confine the work to specific areas, the painters will close off sections[3] of approximately 1,000 square feet per day. Please watch for flags that will mark areas where parking will be[4] unavailable.

While these repairs are being done, please use extra care to avoid accidents. Once the painting[5] has been completed, we will all benefit from the results. We would appreciate your courtesy and patience[6] during the completion of this project. (127)

5

MEMO TO: Richard Mitchell

In accordance with your request, I am enclosing the names of two individuals[1] who might be considered for the position of department supervisor. Please note that each person has some[2] fine qualifications, but neither party has the exact training you specified.

I would like to suggest that[3] we consult the employment agency which helped us locate sales representatives for our special promotion[4] last year. This agency seems to have excellent contacts across the nation, and I believe that we could save a[5] great deal of time by letting the agency make the search for us. If you agree that we need to look outside our[6] company for a supervisor, I would be glad to establish a relationship with this agency.

Please[7] let me know what you wish to do. (146)

LESSON

7

1

MEMO TO: Helen Marshall

Many of our office personnel are saying that our secretarial handbook[1] is out of date. Would you be willing to chair a committee to update the handbook? Your experience as an[2] executive secretary would be extremely valuable. I also know that you are a member of several organizations for[3] secretaries. Perhaps these organizations could contribute timely information to be included in our[4] publication.

I realize that this responsibility is a big addition to your workload, but we[5] might be able to make some adjustments to give you more time. I plan to recommend 10 or 12 other participants[6] for the committee. Could we get together to make some final decisions? (135)

2

Dear Employee:

Welcome to Davis Electronics. You are now part of a firm that has set high standards of[1] excellence in electronic products. We believe that our success is the result of dedicated people[2] working together.

This manual will provide you with guidelines established by our employees. It explains your[3] insurance and retirement programs. It will help you to see how your department fits into the total[4] organization of the company. You will find some benefits which may surprise you. For instance, all of our[5] employees receive discount rates at the health club next to our plant. We also have movie passes available at[6] reduced rates.

Be sure to read this handbook at your earliest opportunity. We hope it represents the beginning[7] of a satisfying career with our firm. Cordially yours, (151)

3

MEMO TO: All Employees

Once again we are pleased to announce

that we will feature special discounts for all[1] employees during our Christmas season. Products from our line of small appliances will be added to your list of[2] possibilities this year. You may also apply the discount to purchases in our toy department.

The items[3] you choose will be sold to you at a discount of 40 percent off the retail price. These sale prices will be[4] available up to December 11, and you may purchase up to a total of $150[5] in merchandise.

We hope our discount plan makes shopping a little easier for you this year. It is our[6] way of wishing you a happy holiday season. (129)

4

Dear Ms. Stevens:

I have been told that your firm produces publications for companies like ours. We are thinking[1] of mailing a monthly newsletter to each of our 400 employees. At the present time we do not have[2] anyone available to write and edit such a newsletter, and it would not be economical to[3] hire additional staff for that purpose.

We have in mind a publication that is three to four pages long. It[4] would contain a few photographs and pieces of artwork. We would like to see articles about individual[5] employees, announcements of coming events, and some national news related to business and industry.[6] Our budget allows us to spend up to 50 cents per copy in production costs.

Is this the kind of[7] periodical you would be interested in producing for us? I would appreciate having your response[8] as soon as possible. Yours very truly, (167)

5

MEMO TO: All Staff

This memo is to clarify our policy regarding office hours during bad weather.[1]

In the event of a heavy snowstorm, please turn the dial on your radio to the university[2] station. If there has been a decision to close our offices or delay opening our offices, that[3] announcement will be made by 7 a.m.

It is not the standard practice of this university to cancel[4] classes because of a heavy accumulation of snow. When classes are held, we expect our offices to[5] continue at the same level of operation.

If you are concerned about the condition of the weather,[6] please listen to the radio. Unless you hear differently, you will be expected to come to work that day.[7] (140)

LESSON ▆▆▆▆▆▆▆▆▆▆▆▆▆

8

1

MEMO TO: Jessica Nelson

I was happy to learn that sales have greatly increased in the retail division.[1] We can now grant your request to add six new staff members to accommodate the current rate of growth and expansion.[2] As you prepare your budget for the next fiscal year, be sure to include these additions with your total request.[3]

I agree with you that this increase is needed. Experience has taught me that the biggest mistake we can[4] make is to understaff our departments. We have always promised to give personal attention to our customers,[5] and we intend to continue that practice. In my opinion, there is no substitute for high quality[6] service.

Keep up the good work. (125)

2

MEMO TO: All Staff

The personnel division is offering something new for your pleasure. We have made arrangements[1] for a number of trips for employees and their families. As you can see from the attached schedule, each trip[2] is about one day in length.

If we receive a positive response to these trips, we will continue to offer[3] them. We encourage you to submit your own travel ideas. Could you suggest some attractions within[4] 150 miles of our plant?

We are also considering a weekend trip to Miami Beach. Please see the[5] enclosed list of hotels and prices. If you are interested in the extended trip, please return the coupon. We[6] still need to determine if this outing should be arranged for adults only or if children are to be included.[7]

We hope you find these plans as exciting as we do. (150)

3

Dear Mr. Thomas:

For many years our employees have started to work at the hour of 8 a.m. Now we are[1] considering a new system. Using the results of a recent study, we are planning to adopt a[2] flexible time schedule. This system would permit each employee to choose his or her own starting time.

Since your firm[3] is already using this type of arrangement, can you answer some questions for us? We would like to know how you[4] introduced this procedure. Do you think it is the best plan? What difficulties have you encountered? Has your level[5] of efficiency increased or decreased as a result?

We anticipate introducing this concept in the[6] near future. Any advice you have would be appreciated. Very truly yours, (135)

4

MEMO TO: All Managers

In a few weeks you will be asked to evaluate the performance of your employees.[1] As preparation for this important event, we will conduct two workshops on how to make successful[2] evaluations. We have also revised the form to be used for each employee.

Evaluation meetings can[3] be a rewarding exercise for both you and your staff. We would like to help you make the most of this opportunity.[4] The workshops will be offered at 1:30 p.m. on October 6 and again at 9:30 a.m.[5] on the following day.

Be sure to attend one of these sessions. They will give you new information on the[6] goals and objectives of management, and they will explain our standards for promotion. We think you will agree that[7] it was time well spent. (144)

5

Dear Mrs. Foster:

Our company has an active service club, and we are looking for a new project to sponsor.[1] I have heard many good things about the volunteer program in your hospital. Could you tell us how it works?[2]

Since we started our service club, participation has grown at a steady rate. We offer several[3] opportunities for employees who wish to volunteer in the community. In order to encourage this[4] kind of involvement, we allow the employees to complete their volunteer obligation during the workday.[5] Unless there are special circumstances, the maximum time allowed each week is two hours.

We would like you to explain[6] your program to our personnel. It might be necessary for us to adapt our plan to fit your schedule, but[7] I am sure that we can find a way to assist you at the hospital. Very truly yours, (156)

LESSON 9

1

Dear Ms. Fields:

Thank you for accepting our invitation. We are extremely pleased that you have agreed to be the[1] guest speaker at our awards banquet.

I hope that you will include some of the material you presented to[2] the personnel managers last month. After I heard your remarks at the national conference, I was determined[3] to bring you before our own group.

We have made the travel arrangements for your visit. The airline ticket is[4] enclosed, and your hotel reservation has been confirmed by our company. I will meet you at the airport and[5] drive you to the hotel. You will have several hours to rest before attending the dinner.

I know that your[6] message will be both helpful and stimulating. Please let me know if I can assist you in any other way. Yours[7] very truly, (143)

2

Dear Mr. Clark:

I understand that you have conducted much research in energy conservation. I have also[1] heard that you examine residences and businesses to determine how efficiently they operate.[2] Could you come to our building to evaluate our level of efficiency?

Since building our plant nine years ago,[3] we have replaced our heating and cooling system with two separate units. Each was designed to accommodate[4] a radius of 6,000 square feet. Now we are concerned that we may be using an excessive amount[5] of electricity. I believe that a complete analysis is in order.

Please call my office to arrange[6] a day for your visit. I will ask the superintendent of our building to set aside the entire day[7] for you. Cordially yours, (144)

3

MEMO TO: Debbie Leonard

We are in the process of designing new identification badges for[1] visitors in our building. You will soon receive a box of identification badges to be used in place[2] of the name tags that we have used in the past. Please give extra attention to distributing and collecting the[3] badges. These items are for permanent use, and we do not wish to create an unnecessary expense by[4] having to replace lost badges.

I know that you supervise several people who take over the reception[5] desk when you are away. Would you please see that each of your assistants understands the procedure for issuing[6] badges?

Proper identification is important to the security of our company. I know that[7] we can count on your support, Debbie. (146)

4

MEMO TO: Customer Service Representatives

Many of you already know that Gloria Hastings will be[1] retiring at the end of this month. Please join us on June 30 for a luncheon in honor of her retirement.[2] The luncheon will begin at 11:30 a.m. in the board room.

Needless to say, this friend and associate[3] will be missed by everyone in our department. Those of us who have had the pleasure of working with her know[4] that she has a special skill for solving difficult problems. Fortunately, she has been very generous[5] in passing her knowledge along to the people working with her.

If you wish to attend the luncheon, please complete[6] and return the enclosed form. We hope that you will gather with us for this very special occasion. (138)

5

Dear Mr. Mason:

We are planning to move into our new offices next month, but I have some doubts about when[1] they will be ready for us. I visited the site this morning, and I am concerned. Is your improvement program[2] on schedule?

Our agreement specifies that the building be completed by March 3. According to the dates[3] listed in the contract, all wir-

ing should have been finished several days ago. You should now be ready to install[4] the flooring and begin painting. Evidently, some valuable time was lost due to bad weather. Do you[5] anticipate making up this lost time?

We are eager to make the transition to the new facility.[6] However, we do not wish to take possession until all construction has been completed. Please advise me right away[7] on when to plan our move. Sincerely yours, (147)

LESSON
10

1

Dear Kevin:

We have often talked about offering assistance to employees who wish to continue their[1] education. There are various ways we can go about accomplishing this. We can pay the tuition fees for[2] those people wishing to enroll in a college nearby. This financial help might be applied to classes held in[3] the evenings. If the course is scheduled by our company as part of job training, however, time would be allowed[4] during the workday. A workshop in word processing or business writing would be an example of this kind of[5] training.

I am investigating the possibility of offering scholarships for employees seeking[6] advanced degrees in their particular areas of study. Engineers and management trainees are[7] representative of this group.

Please think about these ideas. If you think the time is right, I would like to prepare[8] a formal proposal along this line. Sincerely yours, (169)

2

MEMO TO: All Department Heads

You will be glad to know that we are ready to begin the training sessions you[1] have requested. Attached is a list of the programs that have been scheduled so far. More will be forthcoming.

You will[2] find the date and time for each class listed next to the title of each individual topic. We have[3] incorporated most of your suggestions and have added a few of our own.

Among those listed are two sessions[4] that we strongly recommend for everyone. The first is a workshop on how to write effective letters. While I was[5] visiting our plant on the West Coast, I was fortunate enough to attend a similar workshop in Seattle.[6] As a result, my letters have improved greatly.

The class concerning human relations is equally valuable.[7] Both sessions provide training that is fundamental to good management.

Please make your reservations within[8] the periods recommended. We hope that you enjoy the programs. (173)

3

MEMO TO: Office Supervisors

Two weeks ago I sent a memo asking that all vacation schedules be[1] forwarded to my office. I have received approximately half of the total number. Please see that each[2] employee gives you the exact dates he or she has decided upon. It is vital that all scheduling be[3] completed no later than April 6.

Because of the large amount of time and paperwork involved, we must be strict[4] about the deadline for requests. Please remind your staff that those who turn in late schedules may not get their first choice of[5] dates. While we would like to please everyone, we must maintain a minimal number of employees throughout the[6] vacation season. This is necessary to ensure efficiency in our office routine.

I would appreciate[7] your help in this matter. (145)

4

Dear Ms. Ward:

We are interested in the training programs you offer for office staff. Would you be free to talk[1] with me about assembling a plan for us?

We are in the process of installing new equipment throughout our[2] main office building. It is apparent that we must revise our traditional methods of operation.[3]

Perhaps the best way to begin is to have you visit our building. We will show you through our company by[4] introducing you to the various departments and personnel. Due to the changes in our system, we will want[5] you to emphasize procedures used for electronic equipment. However, I am a firm believer in[6] teaching basic skills. Therefore, you should also plan to incorporate other aspects of secretarial training[7] that are equally important.

When you come to our office, we can discuss these things specifically. Please let me[8] know what time would be best for you. Yours very truly, (169)

5

Dear Employees:

Next week we will begin extensive improvements on our building and grounds. We approach this activity[1] with mixed feelings. The remodeling will result in many benefits for everyone, but we will have to[2] endure some inconveniences in the process.

For example, we will probably experience some dust,[3] noise, and general confusion. Although at times it may be difficult, try to concentrate on your work[4] and overlook the activity as much as possible.

We do ask that you take extra care to prevent accidents.[5] Watch where you walk and try to avoid areas under repair.

Naturally, we will do all we can to complete[6] the construction quickly. Thank you for your help during this time. Sincerely yours, (134)

LESSON

11

1

Dear Mrs. Moore:

I have an idea that I am most eager to discuss with you. I think this idea could[1] prove to be very profitable for both of us.

Would you be interested in offering special[2] entertainment to your customers during the lunch hours? I would like to present a style show featuring the latest[3] fashions for women. The arrangement works quite easily if I provide the models and the fashions. We have found this[4] to be a very successful presentation in other eating establishments. Don't you think both of our[5] businesses would benefit from the idea?

If you would like to come to my shop,

we could look at various[6] outfits and determine the kind and quality of clothing that might appeal to your customers. I hope you will share[7] my excitement for trying this idea. Sincerely yours, (151)

2

Dear Miss Grant:

I want to compliment you on your interesting idea for a fashion show. I have shopped in[1] your store often, and I am well acquainted with the excellent quality of merchandise you carry. I think[2] that your suggestion would have appeal for my customers, and I would certainly be willing to work out a plan[3] with you.

I am sure the models you choose are quite professional, and I will leave that choice to your judgment. However,[4] I would like to play a part in selecting the articles of clothing. As you know, we are proud of our patronage[5] here and would like to maintain an image of distinction.

Shall we meet to discuss the details? I will wait for[6] you to call my office. Perhaps we could have lunch here about 1 p.m. and visit your shop afterwards. Yours[7] very truly, (143)

3

MEMO TO: Janet Masters

We will hold a sale on October 15 as a special service to our charge[1] customers. Would you please issue personal invitations to each customer? There are several approaches[2] available to you. Last year we sent notes on small stationery. These cards gave the effect of handwritten notes,[3] and we were extremely pleased with the result.

In previous years we have mailed letters that were typewritten. We have[4] also issued brochures and bulletins. If you have something different in mind, I would welcome your ideas.[5]

It is important that you make our customers feel that this attraction is designed specifically for them. This sale[6] is being closed to the general public, and we are bringing in special merchandise for the sale.

I would be[7] glad to discuss this at your convenience, Janet. (149)

4

Dear Mr. Williams:

Many business executives come to us for help in furnishing their offices. In every[1] single instance in the past, we have produced a surprised and satisfied customer.

Mr. Williams, you should[2] see what a trained, knowledgeable person can do to an unfurnished office. There are methods of defining space[3] that will give an entirely new look to your waiting room. Our designers will help you choose an appropriate image,[4] they will help you make the best use of the space you have available, and they will show you ways of economizing.[5]

When the rooms are finished, you will have an effect that you will feel proud of and that your clients will feel comfortable[6] with. Won't you let us advise you? Sincerely yours, (131)

5

Dear Mrs. Marshall:

Thank you for your letter of June 4. We received the dress you returned to our store, and we have[1] credited your account with the full amount of the purchase.

Our records show that the dress was purchased in April.[2] Unfortunately, our stock of these dresses has been closed out. Since we carry only new merchandise, we must[3] remove all other items with the changing of the season. Therefore, we are unable to give you the same dress[4] in a different size.

It is because of reliable, smart shoppers like you that our store has prospered. Please allow[5] us to continue serving your needs. Cordially yours, (109)

LESSON

12

1

Dear Customer:

We have good news for the businesswoman. We are opening a fashion department just for you.[1]

If you are like the rest of us, you have looked long and hard for appropriate clothing for the office. Many stores[2] make the common mistake of offering stock that is either too formal or not formal enough. Such selections[3] might be fine for a sports event or an afternoon tea, but they are not at all appropriate for the woman[4] executive.

Our new shop will change all that. Don't wait until you are passing by. Make a special trip to examine[5] our inventory. We have suits, dresses, coats, and shoes in designer styles and coordinated colors.[6] Sincerely yours, (122)

2

Dear Mr. Clark:

I am pleased to write this letter on behalf of one of our most dependable customers.[1]

As a wholesale distributor, we have done business with the Mitchell Company for many years. We can certainly[2] testify that this company has paid its bills regularly and promptly. Our records show that most payments were[3] made in advance of the due date in order to take advantage of the cash discount.

As a business manager,[4] Mr. Mitchell demonstrates strong leadership and sound judgment. As an individual, he is known for his fine[5] character. In addition to our business relations, I have worked with this man on various projects in the[6] community and have come to appreciate his interest in social concerns.

I am confident that your[7] bank will be pleased to include this company as one of your treasured customers. Yours very truly, (158)

3

Dear Mr. Lee:

Thank you for your letter of inquiry. We are always delighted to welcome new customers[1] to our growing business.

We carry hundreds of leather items. However, we no longer carry the particular[2] brand you wish to buy. That manufacturer closed its doors about three years ago, and I know of no place where[3] you might find any of the products. If you wish to continue your search, you might try to contact the former[4] owner or his heirs. Although I do not have the exact address, I believe the family still lives on Washington[5] Avenue in the city of Dallas.

If you are interested in other leather goods, I am enclosing[6] our catalog. As you can see, we carry a superior quality of merchandise. We would be glad[7] to be of service to you at any time. Very truly yours, (151)

4

Dear Mr. Jackson:

Please send us 100 units of your No. 879 electric heaters. We[1] would like to have the merchandise immediately. I understand that we will qualify for a discount of[2] 10 percent when we order at least 50 units. Please charge our account accordingly, and I would like you to[3] itemize the discount on the invoice.

I am placing this order at the request of my customers. According[4] to the television commercials, you offer an impressive guarantee with your merchandise. May I assume[5] that you will forward the full details of the warranty with the shipment of merchandise? Since my dealership[6] is relatively new and I have never handled your merchandise, I would appreciate it if you would[7] include literature on your factory policies.

Please let me know when I can expect delivery. Yours[8] truly, (161)

5

Dear Customer:

Many people ask us how we can sell beautiful, quality rugs at half price. The answer is[1] simple. We don't confuse quality with expense.

Because of our large volume of sales in imported rugs, we have[2] lower overhead costs than most competing stores. Because we value our patrons, we pass that savings along in[3] the form of discounted prices.

If you want to add new life to your home without going beyond your budget, pay[4] us a visit. We have area rugs that will dress up your entryway, your dining room, or your fireplace. Don't[5] forget that we also carry the leading brands of carpeting.

Our newest shipment of fall colors is

now on[6] display, and floor samples may be taken out on loan. For quality and service at affordable prices, count[7] on us. Sincerely yours, (144)

LESSON
13

1

Dear Mr. Flint:

To celebrate the anniversary of our grand opening, we have something special in mind[1] for you.

As a charge customer, you already know that we offer quality merchandise at low prices every[2] day. Our regular discount prices eliminate the need for seasonal sales. By shopping in our store, you[3] save money with every purchase you make.

Now we are going to offer you something even better than our[4] everyday low prices. We are inviting you to share a shopping experience that is being reserved[5] exclusively for charge customers. During the entire month of November, you will be entitled to an[6] additional discount of 20 percent on every purchase. Just show your card, and the cashier will make the adjustment[7] on your receipt. Sincerely yours, (145)

2

Dear Mrs. Sylvester:

Thank you for your letter commending our service representatives. We are grateful that[1] you have taken the time to acknowledge our staff. Your letter has been forwarded to the employees who were on[2] duty at the time of your visit.

We have always encouraged our representatives to be considerate[3] toward customers, but we are pleased to hear when someone has been especially helpful and understanding.[4] It is equally rewarding to learn that our customers appreciate these extra efforts to give good service.[5]

We hope you will continue to let us know about your experiences with our establishment. Thank you again[6] for writing. Yours very truly, (126)

3

Dear Sir or Madam:

Once in a great while, a truly rare opportunity comes along. It is our pleasure to[1] bring you the following announcement.

For a limited time only, we will make available to you an[2] outstanding collection of books. These volumes contain the finest selections in literature from America[3] and around the world. Each of the 12 volumes is bound in a hard cover of extraordinary beauty. The set[4] will become an invaluable source of knowledge and entertainment for your whole family.

Because of this[5] special offer, the entire set can be yours for only $129.95. Please[6] remember that the offer expires on January 31, so don't delay. These books are a gift that will[7] increase in value as the years go by. Cordially yours, (149)

4

Dear Mr. and Mrs. Anderson:

Did you know that you can have a new kitchen in your home within 30 days?[1] That's right. You don't have to purchase an expensive new house to have a beautiful kitchen. We can install new[2] cabinets, new sinks, and new appliances in the space your old furnishings now occupy.

Let yourself dream a[3] little. Imagine having all new cabinets in a new wood finish and in a different style. Perhaps you would[4] like to change the layout that you now have. By adding an island cabinet, we can give your kitchen a completely[5] new look. The kitchen shown in the attached photograph can be yours for under $2,000.

If you have[6] questions, come to us for the answers. We will design, build, and install your cabinets with expert care. Sincerely,[7] (140)

5

Dear Member:

The next meeting of our consumer club will be held on September 3. The topic will be a[1] presentation on home furnishings, and we will have samples of new merchandise from the national home show. Indeed,[2] this is your chance to see what will be selling next spring.

You will also be interested in hearing the report[3] on credit practices. The report represents extensive research, and the committee is to be commended[4] for its superior work. We think you will find the results to be both surprising and informative.

If you[5] wish to have your dinner provided, please complete and return the enclosed form. The form will serve as a reservation[6] for you in the event that seating is limited. Yours truly, (132)

LESSON

14

1

Dear Mr. Marvin:

I wish to acknowledge that we received the coat you returned to us. After examin-ing[1] the material carefully, we found that you are correct. There is a small tear in the leather.

The manufacturer[2] is one of the best in the country. It is very rare that we find any problems with clothing from this[3] manufacturer, and perhaps we did not examine the new article as closely as we should have.

Thank you[4] for reminding us that even the finest companies make mistakes. We will watch our merchandise more carefully[5] from now on.

We are sending another jacket to you. We regret that you experienced this inconvenience,[6] and we thank you again for allowing us to correct the situation. Very truly yours, (137)

2

Dear Mrs. Hunter:

When you visited our shop last month, you inquired about buying a bowl or vase that might be[1] used for the center of the table in your dining room. I have been watching for such an item, and I believe[2] I have found the ideal piece.

This bowl is an antique, and it is made of solid silver. It is about 100[3] years old, and it is in perfect condition. Although the bowl is basically simple in design, it has a[4] small band of flowers and leaves around the top. I feel certain that it would be perfect for decorating your dining[5] table.

Mrs. Hunter, when would you like to see this lovely bowl? I am holding it until you can come in.[6] If you decide not to buy it, I would want to put it on display right away. If you would like to call first, I[7] can arrange to be here when you come by. There will be a cup of tea waiting for you. Yours very truly, (159)

3

Dear Mrs. Gregory:

Our store will be happy to cooperate with your hospital in organizing a[1] group of volunteers. The plan you described by phone sounds fine to me, but I would be glad to meet with you to work out[2] the details.

As I understand it, my objective would be to provide the materials you need for decorating[3] the hospital for the Christmas holidays. In addition, you will need someone from my store to design the[4] displays, but you can provide people to assist my employee.

I have someone in mind who has had much[5] experience in creating lovely displays. She is our display manager, Susan Sanderson. She has produced[6] many exciting ideas for us, and I know she would regard this project as very rewarding and[7] challenging.

We are happy to participate in this worthwhile effort. Cordially yours, (155)

4

Dear Mr. Sandifer:

After checking our records carefully, we have found that the amount shown on your most[1] recent billing is correct. The total you now owe is $76.89. We are enclosing[2] copies of the two sales receipts. The first purchase was made in our sporting goods department, and the second was for[3] household items.

During this busy time of the year, it is not unusual for customers to overlook[4] a payment. Now that we have determined the cause of confusion, we know that your account will be brought up to date.[5]

If you have further questions about our billing procedures, please call me personally at 613-2189.[6] Sincerely yours, (124)

5

Dear Ms. Jackson:

Thank you for writing to say that your order has not yet arrived. We do not have a reason for[1] the delay, but we are currently looking into the matter. The evergreen trees were shipped on schedule. They left[2] our loading platform on the same day that we received your request, and they should have reached your residence one week later.[3]

Although we are tracing that shipment, we do not want you to wait any longer for the trees. We are sending[4] a new order today. If you have not received them one week from today, please call me immediately.

We hope[5] you enjoy your beautiful trees, Ms. Jackson. They will add a lovely touch to your yard. Yours truly, (117)

LESSON

15

1

Dear Mr. Davidson:

Thank you for your recent order for sporting goods. Before we can process your order,[1] however, we will need additional information. Our copy of the purchase form shows that you did not include[2] catalog numbers for any of the items requested. Please use the new form that we have enclosed to reorder[3] the merchandise.

Remember to list the quantity for each item, the unit price, and the catalog number.[4] At the bottom of the page, show the total number of items and the total cost of your purchases. Add[5] the shipping fee to this subtotal and show the total amount owed. Be sure your check agrees with the figure for[6] the total amount owed.

We appreciate your patience in correcting this order. We will ship the merchandise[7] as soon as the completed form and payment are received. Yours truly, (152)

2

Dear Ms. Chase:

Enclosed is the extra training manual you requested for your word processor. We have ordered[1] more disks for you, and they are to be mailed directly to your office. You should have them within ten days.

We are[2] delighted to hear that all of the units you rented from us are performing well. The typewriters are among the[3] newest models available in electronic equipment, so I do not anticipate that you will[4] need repair service while you are renting them. However, there is a service center located nearby at[5] 901 Lincoln Boulevard. They will give you prompt and reliable service, and they are accustomed to billing[6] us for such calls.

We hope this arrangement works well for you. Sincerely yours, (132)

3

Dear Mr. and Mrs. Walters:

We are pleased to announce that we are opening a service station in your[1] neighborhood. You have probably driven by the site frequently. It is located at the corner of Fifth Street and[2] Elm Boulevard.

We would like you to join us for free coffee and cake to celebrate our grand opening. Since we are[3] going to be neighbors, we would like to be friends as well. It certainly is an advantage to know the people[4] who service your car.

Our station will carry an extensive line

of automotive parts and accessories. We[5] promise fast and reliable service at economical rates.

Won't you join us on November 8 between[6] 9 a.m. and 9 p.m. for our grand opening? Your attendance would give us great pleasure. Very truly yours,[7] (140)

4

Dear Sir or Madam:

Our new sale catalog is on its way to you. Look for it in the mail.

Please notice that we[1] have expanded many areas, and we have included several other lines that are entirely new this[2] year. For example, check the section on camping gear. We think you will approve of the low prices.

Another[3] exciting addition to our catalog is equipment for water recreation. Wait until you see what is[4] now available.

You will find that this newly published edition of our catalog has grown to twice its[5] original size. Why? We value the patronage of our customers, and we want to offer them the best choices[6] of merchandise.

Avoid making unnecessary trips to shopping centers. Save money the convenient way by[7] ordering at wholesale prices. You can count on us to outfit you to your satisfaction. Variety and[8] dependability have become our specialties. Sincerely yours, (172)

5

Dear Ms. Evans:

The management of our firm requests your presence at a private showing of an exciting[1] collection. It features a favorite American product, designer fashions.

Just when you think you have seen[2] everything, a truly remarkable idea comes along. To prove this point, we are inviting you to view[3] original fashions from the most impressive designers in America.

To make the occasion even more[4] special, we have arranged for entertainment and refreshments. The enclosed card will serve as your invitation. Please[5] show it as you enter our showroom.

It gives us pleasure to host this exclusive showing. We hope you will be our[6] guest. Yours very truly, (124)

LESSON
16

1

Dear Mr. Jackson:

We are enclosing a new identification card for you. Please destroy your old card and[1] replace it with the new card.

As we agreed by telephone, our bank will honor the checks you have written using[2] your full name. In the future, however, be certain that the signature you use on your checks is identical[3] to that shown on your new identification card.

We regret that two of your checks were returned, but our employees[4] reject checks which have not been signed correctly. This is an automatic procedure, and it is designed to[5] protect your account.

Now that you have received your new card, you should have no further difficulty. Yours very[6] truly, (121)

2

Dear Mr. and Mrs. Carlson:

Some people always seem to have the money they need. Did you ever wonder why?[1] The answer is quite simple for our customers. They use our money management service.

By using our management[2] service, you pay yourself before paying your bills. Here is how it works. You begin by depositing your full[3] paycheck in the account. Then we automatically transfer the specified amount into your savings account.[4] You will be amazed at how quickly the account grows.

Perhaps the best part of this plan is its convenience. Our[5] customers insist that they never seem to miss the money that goes into savings. We think it is the most[6] successful plan in banking history.

You can start your management plan today. Call 312-4010 for[7] more information. Very truly yours, (146)

3

Dear Mr. and Mrs. Webb:

As the vacation season approaches, remember to let us make your financial[1] arrangements. You may purchase travel checks at any of our branch offices. As you know, these checks are accepted[2] all over the world. If they are lost or stolen, you can recover the money in a very short time.

If you[3] are planning to stay in one area for a long time, perhaps you should consider a different form of[4] protection. A bank draft or a money order may be more acceptable than individual checks.

The main[5] reasons for vacations are to have fun and to relax. By protecting your finances, we hope to bring you greater[6] peace of mind. Cordially yours, (125)

4

Dear Mr. Hastings:

Because you have long been a customer

of our bank, we invite you to take advantage of[1] a free service. You may use a safe-deposit box at no cost for a period of four weeks.

We shall assign[2] the boxes in the order that requests are received. Therefore, if you have a vacation or trip scheduled, you should[3] give us your dates as soon as possible so that you can be assured of getting your choice of times.

We hope you enjoy[4] this service. These deposit boxes offer the only safe way to protect important papers and possessions.[5] You may even decide to rent one of these deposit boxes on a yearly basis. When you consider[6] the small cost, such protection is very inexpensive. Sincerely yours, (133)

5

Dear Sir or Madam:

We are pleased to announce the opening of our new branch office in your neighborhood.

Our[1] corporation has served millions of customers all over the country. We have made it possible for families[2] like yours to realize their dreams. We have helped them achieve home ownership, vacations, college educations, and[3] other special needs. Because our payment plans are so reasonable, they have eased the burden of repaying loans.[4]

When you need financial assistance, you should choose a lending company as carefully as you would choose a doctor.[5] Ask your friends about us or bring your questions to us personally.

To learn more about our services, pay[6] us a visit. Our account managers, the most helpful people in town, will be delighted to meet you. Yours[7] truly, (141)

LESSON ▬▬▬▬▬▬
17

1

Dear Mr. Wilson:

Here is the brochure you requested describing our retirement account. Everyone has[1] different needs. It would be most helpful to you to meet with one of our staff members to discuss your individual[2] situation. We can make an appointment at your convenience.

We have included an application form[3] with this letter. If you have already decided on a particular option, just fill out the form and return[4] it to us in the envelope we have provided. Your new account will become active in approximately[5] ten days.

Please let us know if there is anything more we can do for you. Sincerely yours, (116)

2

Dear Ms. Russell:

Are you taking advantage of all that your bank offers you? For example, where do you now keep[1] your valuable papers? Are you protecting your insurance policies and other important items?

Why[2] not allow us to keep them for you in a safe, convenient place? You can store them in your own safe-deposit box[3] for a small amount per year. The process is as simple as it is safe. In five minutes you can transfer your[4] valuables to a place that is actually safe from fire and theft. Yet, you will have easy access to these[5] possessions whenever you desire.

Let us show you how it is done. Dial our

bank number, 217-2211,[6] for more information. Our service representative will give you the full details. Very truly yours,[7] (140)

3

Dear Mrs. Clay:

We were delighted to receive your request for credit, and we are enclosing an application[1] form. Since you will be coming to our city from another state, you will need to complete the form and return[2] it in the envelope that we have supplied.

Your application will be processed immediately. As soon as[3] your line of credit has been established, your credit card will be on its way to you.

We are pleased to welcome you[4] to our community, Mrs. Clay, and we look forward to serving you on a regular basis. Please call on[5] us for all of your banking needs. Sincerely yours, (109)

4

MEMO TO: Nancy Parker

We are considering a new system for issuing bank receipts. You probably[1] recall that this system was discussed at the national conference in Las Vegas. Many of the major banks in[2] the country no longer issue monthly statements that list each transaction item by item. Instead, they include[3] a brief list showing the total amount of withdrawals, the total deposits, and the balance of the account.[4] This summary is included with the canceled checks.

It has been suggested that we look at this system very[5] closely. If the plan seems appropriate for our bank, we may wish to use it. A meeting is tentatively[6] scheduled for Thursday at 9 a.m. Please

be prepared to give your reactions to the enclosed proposal.[7] (140)

5

Dear Miss Lee:

We are inviting members of our community to serve on a panel at our next general[1] meeting. The topic to be discussed is the economic future of our city. Would you be willing to[2] participate?

As a vice president of the largest bank in this area, you would contribute much to the[3] event. We would like to hear your views on the future of interest rates and the availability of money[4] in general. In addition, we will be asking for suggestions on attracting new industries to this part[5] of the state.

Other members on the panel will represent the areas of real estate, industry, and local[6] government. I hope you will accept our invitation, Miss Lee. Perhaps the enclosed agenda will help to[7] guide you in making a decision. Yours truly, (149)

LESSON
18

1

Dear Dr. Foster:

We are hearing much about the advantages of investing money in mutual funds.[1] However, have you asked yourself about the safety of these funds? A promise is not a guarantee. Interest[2] rates for mutual fund companies are good today, but six months from now they may be much lower.

On the other[3] hand, we can offer you

something more dependable. When you invest in a certificate of deposit at[4] our savings and loan institution, you get high interest rates that are guaranteed not to change. You need not worry[5] about the safety of your deposit because the money is insured by the federal government.

We[6] cordially invite you to investigate further. Call or come by one of our convenient branch offices. Sound[7] planning makes good sense. Yours very truly, (147)

2

Dear Sir or Madam:

Do you lose precious time going from place to place to pay your bills? Did you know that Central Bank[1] will perform that service for you?

If you open an executive account with us, we will pay your bills[2] automatically on the assigned day of each month. How does this handy system work? With a minimum balance of[3] $3,000, you will pay no monthly service charge for the bills paid under the executive plan. For each[4] additional check you write, you pay only a small fee. At the end of each six-month period, you will receive an[5] itemized receipt for your tax records.

Our executive account is only one of many convenient[6] services at Central Bank. We put your dollars and cents to work for you. Respectfully yours, (136)

3

Dear Henry:

I am enclosing the information you requested to bring your budget up to date. Please note that[1] the account reference number is 63003. It should be used for all expenses related to the[2] fund drive.

Please accept our sincere thanks for serving as chairman this year. You provided the kind of leadership[3] needed to make this event the most successful one in history.

There are many areas of success we can[4] point to. You provided ideas that were imaginative, you set a tone of friendliness and eagerness,[5] and you organized the drive in such a way that volunteers could meet their goals.

On behalf of the entire[6] community, I am expressing gratitude for half a million people. You certainly deserve it for a job well[7] done. Sincerely, (143)

4

Dear Miss James:

It has been brought to my attention that you have not used your charge account since November of last year.[1] Have you considered all the ways that your charge card can make life easier for you?

For example, using our charge[2] card means that you do not have to carry large sums of cash with you. In addition, our charge system provides you with[3] permanent records of each expenditure you make. There are still other advantages. If you are in a hurry[4] and cannot stop by the store, you can call in your order. Charging a purchase can be done by telephone as[5] quickly and as easily as it can be done in person.

Your credit card was designed to make shopping more[6] efficient for you. Remember to use it often. Yours very truly, (132)

5

Dear Dr. and Mrs. Webb:

Thank you for your letter requesting advice on how to set up a trust account.

As[1] we discussed by phone, I will be glad to answer your questions when we meet next week. You are wise to consider your[2] future now. In the complex area of finance, good planning makes a major difference in how you live a few[3] years from now.

I suggest that we begin by taking a detailed, careful look at your assets and liabilities.[4] We should also consider the tax advantages available to you. Since there are various trust plans[5] available, we will want to choose the one most appropriate for you and your family.

Please remember[6] to bring the financial data we discussed. Yours very truly, (131)

LESSON

19

1

Dear Mr. and Mrs. Evans:

We are pleased to grant you the mortgage you applied for. We received responses from[1] all of the references you listed, and your credit rating has been approved.

Since I am your financial[2] advisor, I have already contacted your realtor and the current owners of the property which you are[3] purchasing. A closing date will be set within the next ten days, and you will be notified of the exact date[4] and time.

If you have additional questions between now and the time for closing, please feel free to talk with me at[5] any time. We are delighted to give you this happy news, and we look forward to assisting you in purchasing[6] your new home. Yours truly, (125)

2

Dear Mr. and Mrs. Grant:

All of us have the responsibility of planning for our families. If our[1] estates are to be distributed properly, we must review our wills frequently. We should revise them as often[2] as necessary to keep them current.

Making decisions about our estates can be very difficult.[3] That is why it is so important to have the advice of a financial expert. Our advisors will help you[4] make the kinds of decisions that will protect your family. They will relieve you of the doubts that result from[5] unfinished business. Knowing that your family is safe and secure, you can then live your lives with a sense of[6] satisfaction and contentment.

Talk with us soon about your future. We are specialists in the planning of estates.[7] Sincerely yours, (142)

3

Ladies and Gentlemen:

You are cordially invited to be our guests at the grand opening of our newest[1] branch bank. It is located in Northside Shopping Center near Interstate 70 at the Grandview exit.

Help[2] us celebrate by having coffee and cookies with us from 10 a.m. to 5 p.m. on September 5. We[3] would enjoy meeting you, and we would like to help you get acquainted with our banking services. Our personnel[4] will be on hand to greet you personally and answer any questions you might have.

May we count on having you[5] attend? We are eager to become a part of this growing neighborhood, and we hope you will give us this[6] opportunity to express our appreciation in person. Yours truly, (133)

4

Dear Mr. Baxter:

We are about to celebrate a very special anniversary. For 25 years[1] we have managed investments for citizens of this town. Now we wish to let everyone know how much we have[2] appreciated knowing and serving them.

Today our assets are in excess of $50 million. Without[3] a doubt, we owe a debt of thanks to this community for our growth and prosperity. Will you help us celebrate?[4]

Join us for a tribute on May 17. The mayor of our city will be in attendance to accept[5] our pledge to the city. We will also renew our pledge to bring exciting opportunities to our clients.[6]

We will look forward to seeing you here. Very truly yours, (131)

5

Dear Dr. and Mrs. Gregory:

We are pleased to make an announcement regarding an improvement in services[1] for you. You will no longer receive a lengthy statement every month as you have in the past. Instead, you will[2] receive a brief statement showing the total withdrawals, total deposits, and current balance of your account.[3] This statement will be accompanied by your canceled checks.

We are adopting this new system because it[4] eliminates the need for an itemized listing of your banking activities. The change will result in greater[5] efficiency for you as well as for us. We will continue to offer you, a customer we value highly,[6] banking services at no additional cost to you.

If you should have questions regarding your own records or[7] our statements, we will be happy to answer them. Cordially yours, (151)

LESSON 20

1

Dear Mr. and Mrs. Harper:

Many people are asking themselves how they will be able to afford to send[1] their children to college. Costs rise every year, and there is less and less aid available.

We may have the answer[2] for you. With our plan for educational assistance, you design the kind of financial aid you need. You may[3] establish a line of credit and draw against it for college expenses, or you may take out a loan each year[4] in which you need help. Because of a government program, we can offer you special interest rates that are less[5] than other lending rates.

If you have a son or daughter who is rapidly approaching the college years, let us[6] help. Serving you is our most important concern. Yours truly, (131)

2

Dear Mr. Billings:

We will be pleased to review your application for a loan for your business. As we discussed[1] by phone, you will need to fill out an additional form if the loan is for agricultural equipment.[2] I am enclosing the necessary papers. Please be certain to give full details for each question asked.

We will[3] also need to see proof of your annual income. Please include a copy of your federal tax statements for the[4] past three years. It would also be helpful if you would supply a list of the machines that you plan to purchase. It[5] will expedite the processing of your loan if you include model numbers and prices.

We will make every[6] effort to have an answer for you by the time you requested. Thank you for your patience in this matter, Mr.[7] Billings. Very truly yours, (145)

3

Dear Depositor:

For many years our Christmas club has been popular with our clients. This year we are going[1] a step further. We are creating a similar kind of account to help pay for vacation expenses.

There[2] are many reasons for opening such an account. Just as the Christmas club has eased your shopping expenses, the[3] vacation club will make your trip a happier experience for everyone. The plan provides a steady,[4] convenient way to set aside the money you need for family fun.

Listen to this important bonus. Members[5] will become eligible for discounts on trips here and abroad. Your discounts will include reductions on air fares,[6] hotel accommodations, and other attractions.

Do you want to hear more? Return the enclosed card without[7] delay. Start your account now and let the fun begin. Cordially yours, (151)

4

Dear Miss Robinson:

After reviewing your records with care, we have found no error in your checking account.[1] We must assume, therefore, that the balance shown on your statement is correct.

Since your records do not agree with the[2] statement, would you like to bring your checkbook to our office? A service representative can then go over your[3] register with you. Occasionally, we find that a deposit has been overlooked or a withdrawal has been[4] recorded incorrectly. There is also the possibility that an error in calculation has occurred.[5]

Please visit us at any time during regular banking hours. We are always happy to be of assistance.[6] Yours very truly, (124)

5

Dear Mr. Temple:

I want to tell you how much my family and I appreciate the work of your teller,[1] Marsha Carter.

My mother is quite elderly, and she has very poor vision. However, she insists upon[2] being as independent as possible, and we have tried to respect her wishes. As you can probably[3] imagine, handling financial matters is very difficult for her. That is where your teller, Ms. Carter,[4] has been such a help to us.

She is always kind, considerate, and helpful toward my mother. As a result,[5] we have all come to rely upon her. We are very grateful for her patience and warm personality. Sincerely,[6] (121)

LESSON ▨▨▨▨▨▨▨

21

1

Gentlemen:

Insurance companies, which probably represent an important part of your sales every year, hire[1] more office employees than most other industries do. They also require more office supplies than other types[2] of businesses. As a manufacturer of paper goods, are you aware that you can reach all of the major[3] insurance companies by advertising in our monthly report?

Our report goes into the mail on the[4] eleventh day of each month. The readership for our publication is estimated to be very high among[5] the top executives in this field. To show you why our report is so popular, we are including a[6] sample copy with this letter. This enclosure will open the door to a giant market just waiting for you.[7]

Please keep the entire copy for future reference. Someone from our firm will contact you in a few days to answer[8] any questions you may have. Sincerely yours, (168)

2

Dear Dr. and Mrs. Brown:

Everyone plans on having good health and a good life. However, the main provider[1] in the family must see to it that the family is protected in all kinds of situations. Although[2] none of us likes to think that unfortunate things might happen, we each need to know that the welfare of our family[3] is in safe hands if an accident or illness does occur.

Choosing the right policy can be a difficult[4] task. To make the right decision, you really need the advice of an expert. When you are working with a friend[5] who knows what policies are available and understands the needs of your family, you can rely upon[6] the advice that person gives.

Please allow me to act as that friend. I have had 13 years of experience, and[7] I have a brand new policy to offer. I would welcome the opportunity to tell you more about it.[8] Very truly yours, (164)

3

Dear Homeowner:

Do you wonder how some insurance companies can offer coverage at low prices? Perhaps[1] it has something to do with the way they respond to claims. For example, do these companies ever mention the[2] performance of their claims departments?

Our company is proud of its reputation for processing claims. With[3] Mutual Farm as your insurance company, you will always come first. To help prove this point, I am enclosing a[4] recent article. It shows that we are rated at the top of the list in paying claims. In a recently published[5] survey, our clients indicated that we offer settlements which are fair to all concerned.

Isn't it time[6] for you to take a good look at a company you can depend upon? Call our toll-free number today. Yours[7] truly, (141)

4

Dear Sandra:

This letter is to acknowledge your help in settling the claim filed by your client, Andrew Davis.[1] I am aware of how complex and complicated this matter could have become. You demonstrated much skill in[2] organizing and filing the claim. In addition, you provided much support to the insured parties. By doing[3] your job well, you have represented this company very well.

Yours is the type of performance that has made[4] this company famous. I know that we can count on you to continue to set an example for other agents.[5]

Again, Sandra, you have my sincere thanks for exhibiting excellence in your daily work. Cordially yours,[6] (120)

5

Dear Mr. and Mrs. Mason:

After reviewing the policy that covers your home and personal property,[1] I have some suggestions. Could we plan to talk sometime in the next few days?

When you purchased your homeowner insurance,[2] it was adequate for your needs. Since the date you took out that policy, however, two significant[3] changes have taken place. You have added several improvements, and inflation has affected the worth of your[4] home. As a result, your house has increased greatly in value.

You would be wise to protect that worth by upgrading[5] your insurance. There are some options that will give you added protection for a very modest increase in rates.[6] It will take only a few minutes to go over these options, and I will be happy to work around your[7] schedule.

I will plan to call you one afternoon this week to establish a time. Sincerely yours, (156)

LESSON 22

1

Dear Parents:

Is every member of your family covered by your current insurance policy? You would be[1] surprised at how many people answer that question incorrectly. Because their policies were adequate[2] several years ago, they automatically assume that the coverage is as good today as it was[3] yesterday.

All too often we overlook an important consideration. When children go away to college,[4] they may no longer be covered under some family plans. Don't let this oversight happen to you. We can provide[5] you with a policy that will insure your sons and daughters while they are traveling to and from college.

While[6] living on campus, your children will be protected in the event of illness or injury. They will also be[7] protected against the loss of personal property due to theft or fire.

This is an ideal way to supplement[8] your existing coverage. If you would like to have more information, send us the enclosed card today.[9] Cordially yours, (182)

2

Dear Mrs. Morgan:

Thank you for your letter asking about the health benefits you now have. I think I can answer[1] all of your questions.

Use the regular patient claim form, which is yellow, for all charges that you incur as[2] an out-patient. Do not use this form for dental claims. A separate form, which is gray in color, should be obtained[3] from your business office. It will contain a different set of instructions for submitting requests.

Please remember[4] that a separate form must be filed for each insured party. Make copies of your receipts and keep them in your[5] records for tax purposes.

Always feel free to call us any weekday between 9 a.m. and 5 p.m.[6] Sincerely yours, (122)

3

Dear Miss Webster:

This is a reminder that your premiums are now overdue. According to the terms of your[1] contract, your policy will expire if payment is not received by January 15.

Are you aware of[2] what it would cost to replace that policy at current rates today? If you permit your policy to lapse, you[3] will never again be able to obtain insurance at such a low cost. Every year that you wait will move you[4] into a higher age bracket. For every year that you wait, you will pay higher premiums.

Miss Webster, don't[5] allow your policy to be canceled. Mail us your payment today so that your security will be protected.[6] Let us work together to keep your policy in force. Respectfully yours, (134)

4

MEMO TO: Alex Long

I have finished reading your report, and I was very impressed with your recommendations.[1] I agree with you that we should offer a group plan for members of private organizations.

Of course, it[2] would be necessary to include only those organizations that operate on a national basis[3] and have a large enough membership to support this kind of insurance plan. Could you provide a list of those[4] organizations? Among the examples you listed were auto clubs and travel clubs. These are excellent[5] suggestions. I would also guess that there are several groups that collect specific items. For example, people[6] who collect stamps or coins might be candidates for our policy.

You have presented an exciting opportunity[7] for us in an area we have long been interested in. Congratulations on your findings, Alex.[8] (160)

5

Dear Sir:

Have you often been frustrated by an inability to obtain group protection for your employees?[1] If the answer is yes, then we have good news for you and other small companies.

If you have at least 50[2] employees, your firm may qualify for the benefits of one of our group plans. We have made them flexible enough[3] to apply to a wide range of businesses. You will find that our options are among the best available.[4] Choose from policies covering dental, major medical, whole life, or accidental death insurance.

Learn more[5] about us. The enclosed card, which we have provided for your convenience, should be completed and mailed to us for[6] more information. When it is a matter of building a better future, there is no better time to begin[7] than the present. Act now. Yours truly, (146)

LESSON 23

1

Dear Mr. Henderson:

I am enclosing the file of one of our employees. Attached to the file is a patient[1] claim form, which we hope you can process immediately.

It usually takes about ten days to process[2] one of these claims. In this special instance, however, I hope that we can accomplish the task much sooner. This[3] employee will be hospitalized for more than two weeks. He has already paid a substantial amount to his[4] doctor, and he has also paid several laboratory expenses.

The patient recently purchased this cash[5] policy as a supplement to his other coverage. Although the paperwork is not yet final, this[6] employee was covered from the moment he signed the policy. It pays $50 per day, and it would be a[7] great help to him now. Very truly yours, (146)

2

Dear Ms. Gray:

Are you paying too much for auto insurance? Although you may find it hard to believe, most adult[1] drivers do pay excessive rates. Do you know why they make this unfortunate mistake? It is because they do not[2] take the time to shop around for the lowest possible rates.

Check our rates and compare them with the rates of other[3] companies. You will not find better rates for comprehensive, collision, or liability insurance.[4] That isn't all. There is a bonus for safe drivers. If you have not had an accident during the last five years,[5] you may qualify for an additional discount.

We are happy to provide you with this news, Ms. Gray. A[6] representative will call soon to answer questions and tell you more about our company. Yours very truly,[7] (140)

3

Dear Ed:

The enclosed article appeared recently in a popular business publication, *Business Update.*[1] Please read it and tell me what you think about the executive plan that is described in the story.

As you know,[2] we have often considered adopting a new insurance portfolio for business executives. Although[3] we would not wish to duplicate this exact plan, I would like to see us offer a similar arrangement. In[4] order to offer a portfolio that is properly balanced, we need to expand into other areas[5] of financial planning. I suggest that we create an advisory service that can contribute this kind[6] of input.

I am sure this week is particularly busy for you, but I would like to discuss this idea[7] by tomorrow or the day after. Sincerely, (149)

4

Dear Betty:

I am responding to the message you left on my answering machine. Although I attempted to[1] return your call several times, I was unable to reach you. Therefore, I am enclosing some information[2] for your consideration.

The enclosed packet describes our plan for disability insurance. Since you are[3] self-employed and are the sole support of your children, this policy would be excellent for you. Please give it[4] serious thought.

When you are ready to discuss it further, call my office. I can arrange to see you within[5] a day or two. If I haven't heard from you by next week, Betty, I will call again. This is an important matter[6] for you, and you are very wise to seek a solution. Sincerely yours, (133)

5

Dear Mr. North:

I am returning the claims you filed on April 9 for medical charges. According to our[1] records, claims for those expenses have already been received by our office. They were filed by the provider of[2] the services, and a check will be issued to the attending physician.

When the above payment is made, you[3] will receive an acknowledgment from this office informing you of the sum paid toward this claim. If there are still[4] unpaid charges, your physician will bill you for the amount still owed.

If you would like an additional[5] explanation of benefits, contact this office directly. Cordially yours, (113)

LESSON ▰▰▰▰▰▰▰▰
24

1

Dear Ms. Doyle:

I would be pleased to be the speaker at your luncheon on October 4. The topic of my address[1] will be "Investment Planning."

As you suggested in your correspondence, many people do not fully understand[2] the role of their insurance agent. The agent can help them choose investments that will increase their income after[3] retirement. Most companies offer a variety of annuities, and the rate of interest is[4] competitive with private funds. It is my opinion that annuities are usually a safer[5] investment.

I will talk for approximately 15 minutes, and then I will allow time for questions from the[6] audience. Since the meeting begins promptly at noon, I will arrange to be there about 20 minutes before then.[7] Thank you for your invitation. Sincerely yours, (149)

2

Dear Mr. Clay:

Thank you for your letter complimenting the work of our assistant, Jennifer Hastings. Everyone[1] here in the claims division knows that she takes more than an

ordinary interest in her work. It is always[2] rewarding to hear from clients who have made the same observation.

It takes a very special person to[3] fill the role of a claims assistant. Many of these people are still at their desks long after the normal workday[4] has ended. This dedication makes it possible for us to act upon claims immediately. Such service[5] results in efficiency for our company and peace of mind for our clients.

We appreciate your taking[6] the time to comment on your pleasant experience. Such encouragement helps our staff to maintain the excellence[7] that is characteristic of this firm. Very truly yours, (151)

3

Dear Mr. Harper:

When I was in Tulsa last week, I heard some news that will be of interest to you. Evidently,[1] a merger is being planned for two major insurance companies. United Life and General Group will[2] soon become one company. Negotiations are currently underway, and we can expect an announcement[3] any day now from the presidents of those companies.

As a result of this merger, the new firm will become[4] one of the largest insurance companies in the nation. The combined assets of the two companies total[5] several billion dollars. Attached is a newspaper article which indicates that their holdings are both[6] diversified and extensive.

I will be eager to see what develops from this new leadership in the[7] insurance community. Yours truly, (146)

4

Dear Mrs. Tower:

Happy birthday! It is a pleasure to send

you my best wishes on this special occasion.[1]

It also gives me pleasure to thank you for continuing your policies with our company. I have always[2] felt that the main reason people choose one insurance company over another is because of the agent[3] with whom they work. If you have confidence in the agent, you know you can rely upon the company that he[4] or she represents.

I am happy to say that I have made many friends since becoming an agent, and I enjoy[5] handling the insurance needs of those friends. I am sure you realize that you may call on me any time[6] you need help.

I hope you enjoy many happy returns. Very truly yours, (134)

5

Dear Mr. Wilson:

It was pleasant having breakfast with you yesterday, and I enjoyed our discussion thoroughly.[1] You have some excellent ideas on the subject of annuities, and I would like to consider them[2] further. Perhaps it is time I revised my insurance portfolio.

I see no need for additional[3] coverage in the area of personal injury or public liability. I believe that my[4] supplementary policy provides adequate protection for various types of liability. On the[5] other hand, I am attracted to the investment plans you mentioned. I would like to consider enrolling both[6] of my children, who are currently in college and soon will be supporting themselves.

Why don't you give me a call?[7] I would like to talk with you again soon. Sincerely, (149)

LESSON

25

1

Dear Mr. Marshall:

Enclosed is a check for $950 to reimburse you for the theft of your[1] home entertainment system. As you know, the deductible amount of your insurance is $200.[2] That amount has already been deducted from the value of your stolen goods.

In estimating the total[3] amount of the loss, we generally use a scale of 10 percent per year to arrive at a fair rate of[4] depreciation. However, your sales receipt indicates that the set was less than two months old. Therefore, we are[5] treating the set as brand new merchandise, and you will not be charged a fee for depreciation.

We are sorry[6] that you suffered this loss. It represents a disappointment and an inconvenience for you. We are happy to make[7] this settlement for you, and we wish you well in the future. Very truly yours, (154)

2

Dear Mr. George:

The rising cost of college tuition is already out of reach for a lot of people. Have[1] you thought about enrolling in a plan that will help pay for college educations?

Because your children are young,[2] you still have time to prepare for the responsibilities that lie ahead. You can design your own annuity[3] plan that will help defray college expenses. Ordinarily, the amount you pay will depend upon the[4] ages of your children, on your age, and on the total amount you wish to accumulate. You may make payments[5] on a monthly, quarterly, or annual basis.

Act now for the future, Mr. George. When the need arrives, your[6] finances will be in a strong position. You will be ready to meet this need. Yours very truly, (138)

3

Dear Mrs. Miller:

I have reviewed the file you submitted regarding your claim for dental services. Our[1] repayment schedule is shown on the attached page next to the itemized list of expenses.

Before filing future[2] claims, you may wish to review your dental policy. You and each of your insured family members are entitled[3] to one routine examination and cleaning per year. Your dental plan can also be applied to some forms[4] of oral surgery and treatment for the gums. Surgery for the jaw, however, does not fall in the dental[5] category. We suggest that you resubmit the bill as a claim against your major medical insurance.[6]

In regard to your other questions, Mrs. Miller, part of the costs of dental appliances will be shared by[7] your insurance. The amount of coverage depends upon the specific treatment. Sincerely yours, (158)

4

Dear Homeowners:

Now that you own that lovely home you dreamed of, protect it for your family. If something should happen[1] to one of you, would the rest of your family be forced to sell the house?

For a minimal payment each month,[2] they can be assured of never losing their home. Mortgage insurance is a bargain, and we can show you why. For[3] as little as $9.95 per month, you will be free of worries about providing for your[4] family in case of an early death or disability. Many policies cover the husband only, but[5] we have options that apply to both owners. For families that depend upon two incomes, it is just as[6] important to insure the wife as it is to insure the husband.

Won't you take this important step today? For the[7] name of an agent near you, call us free of charge. Very truly yours, (152)

5

Dear Ms. James:

You are probably aware that many insurance companies reserve the right to adjust their rates[1] within a given year. Of course, this adjustment often results in a rate increase at your expense.

We operate[2] differently. We believe that you are paying enough for automobile insurance when you renew the[3] policy each year. We don't believe in springing surprises on our clients. Once you purchase a policy, it[4] is yours for a full year. Unless you alter the conditions of your policy, the rates will not change.

Return the[5] enclosed form, and you will receive a rate quotation. If you would like a salesperson to call on you, check the[6] appropriate box on the form. Otherwise, you will not be contacted. Respectfully yours, (136)

LESSON

26

1

Dear Investor:

Is this a good time to buy stocks for future growth? The answer is yes. When you invest, you should locate[1] stocks that will yield a reasonable profit over a long period of time. We can suggest some fine examples[2] of leadership companies that are now available on the stock exchange.

The attached chart shows what has[3] happened to common stocks in the recent past. Of course, we cannot expect the same trends to continue. That is where[4] our specialists will be of help to you.

In order to be reliable, a broker must be a trained expert.[5] He or she should always be available to advise you about when to sell, buy, trade, or hold. Our brokers will[6] provide that counsel.

For many of our customers, common stocks make common sense. Why not call us today? Very[7] truly yours, (142)

2

Dear Mr. Gregory:

There are many reasons for trusting us with your financial security. In addition[1] to the protection that we are required to give you by law, we can now insure your account for an additional[2] $250,000. We also carry millions of dollars of protection against the loss[3] of securities by fire, theft, or natural disaster.

You get all this protection along with the[4] personalized service and professional advice that we have been offering for almost 100 years. Call and[5] ask to speak to one of our counselors. We will be glad to help you outline an investment plan that is practical[6] for you. Cordially yours, (125)

3

Dear Ms. Christopher:

Knowing how much to save and when to invest can be very difficult for most people. During[1] this time of economic uncertainty, financial planning is particularly confusing. One thing[2] is certain, however. If you are to have a better future, saving and investing are essential.

How do[3] you arrive at a reasonable balance between safety and return on your dollars? Our firm is here to help[4] you make the right decisions. We provide guidelines that provide security while also allowing for a[5] considerable profit.

To help you get started, we are conducting a series of classes in finance. The[6] enclosed brochure contains all the information you need to enroll. Won't you take this important step today? Yours[7] truly, (141)

4

Dear Mr. and Mrs. Bishop:

Welcome to our family of shareholders. Because we want to keep you fully[1] informed about the company's status, we are enclosing literature that describes our activities from[2] the past year.

Included in this packet is a copy of our latest report. If you would like to receive copies[3] of past reports, we will gladly send them to you upon request.

When you are in the vicinity of our[4] plant, we invite you to visit our modern facilities. It is fascinating to see the electronic[5] equipment and computerized methods now in operation. Our public relations department gives guided[6] tours daily through the plant.

The outlook for our business is very bright, and we anticipate that this will be an[7] equally profitable year. Cordially yours, (149)

5

Dear Ms. Conway:

You are correct. An investment that yields high returns is a risk, but it is also an exciting[1] opportunity. Such an investment can take off with supersonic speed, or it can fall with a thud. How[2] do you know when to take a chance?

We like to recommend a compromise that has worked well for a number of[3] investors. We evaluate the growth of companies that have demonstrated solid progress over a number[4] of years. These are firms with strong management and a willingness to defer quick profits for solid advancement. Stocks[5] such as these yield profits over a long term.

We can help you identify these stocks. Since your financial[6] situation prevents you from gambling on quick profits, you are more likely to feel safe with this predictable,[7] steady rate of return. Sincerely, (146)

LESSON

27

1

Dear Mr. and Mrs. Turner:

We are proud to include you among our new shareholders. We appreciate the[1] confidence you have shown in us by investing in our company.

Enclosed is a brief history of our[2] company. We are proud of our heritage, and we are just as proud of the contribution we have made to the[3] automotive industry. Since introducing our first product more than 70 years ago, we have established[4] a reputation for innovation and dependability. Although that first engine was very different[5] from the machinery now being manufactured, it reflected the research and fine craftsmanship that would[6] earn us top billing in a world market.

We welcome you as partners in the growth and development of our[7] corporation. When you are in this area, please make it a point to visit our headquarters. You are now a part[8] of us. Very truly yours, (165)

2

Dear William:

I am attaching a memo written by the director of our international division.[1] It contains a brief summary of our existing accounts and recent transactions with banks that are located[2] overseas. As you can see from the report, our banking affiliate in Paris is one of the most active[3] underwriters of foreign currency in the world. Perhaps we should consider consolidating our foreign[4] loans and making this bank our primary agent.

Please read the memo and give me your reactions to the[5] recommendations outlined on page 4. It is time to make a decision regarding future interests, and[6] I would like to discuss several ideas with you before we attend the meeting that has been scheduled for[7] 10 o'clock on Tuesday.

I will be most eager to have your reply. Sincerely, (153)

3

Dear Roy:

Thank you for sending me a copy of the financial report. I was particularly pleased to learn[1] that capital gains overseas have increased more than 6 percent during this fiscal year. Because of the obvious[2] success of our existing policies, I see no reason to make major changes in our investment holdings.[3]

I, too, am encouraged by the stability of the American dollar currently in evidence[4] in Western Europe. Our foreign assets are approaching $2 billion at this time. This information[5] indicates that we are experiencing a period of economic growth, and I believe that we should[6] discuss additional avenues of expansion abroad.

I have appointments scheduled for 9 a.m. and[7] 2:30 p.m. tomorrow. Any other time would be fine for me to meet with you. Cordially yours, (157)

4

MEMO TO: Bill Michaels

I have asked that reminders be sent to all of our clients regarding the series of[1] lectures beginning in October. These sessions will deal specifically with personal finance, and they will cover[2] a broad range of investments. Topics will include risks and benefits, savings and loan practices, stock options,[3] insurance plans, and future bond yields.

As you requested, I am enclosing copies of the proposal for our[4] dividend reinvestment plan. You are quite right about its potential. This is an excellent opportunity[5] to show our members that they can reinvest dividends in company stock without paying fees to brokers.[6]

I believe that many people will want to take advantage of this exceptional opportunity. (139)

5

Dear Dr. Cox:

Thank you for your letter of March 7. We are pleased that you have indicated an interest[1] in our company's reinvestment plan. Certainly, this is an excellent time to apply your dividends toward[2] the purchase of additional shares.

To determine your eligibility, please refer to the enclosed[3] guidelines. If you still wish to participate in the plan, please send us the name and registration number listed[4] on your stock certificate. We will send you an authorization form as soon as we receive the information[5] listed above. Once you have completed and returned the form to us, we will be able to enroll you in the[6] plan.

Thank you again for your interest in our company. Sincerely yours, (134)

LESSON

28

1

Dear Board Member:

I am writing to express my opinion about the proposed plan to sell the textile mill. I[1] believe that an adjustment in the tariffs will be made by the federal government to allow for additional[2] imports of materials. If there is hope for the mill to get back to normal production, we should apply[3] for a loan and look for a new market.

Are you convinced that we must choose between selling or losing everything?[4] Why don't you investigate new fabrics which could combine raw wool with other natural fibers? Although there[5] is a shortage of natural materials, the demand for manufactured goods is higher now than ever[6] before. I suggest that we open up a new line and allow the plant to continue production at the[7] normal level.

There must be a solution to ensure that this business continues to operate. Let us find it.[8] Yours very truly, (164)

2

Dear Mr. Kingston:

This is in response to your inquiry about transferring the ownership of stocks from one[1] individual to another.

The process of changing a title is fairly simple. You should first complete[2] the form that is presented on the reverse side of the security. Be sure to fill in all the information[3] requested. You must then ask an officer of a bank to authenticate your signature. There is a small[4] fee associated with the transfer of each share of stock.

Forward the certificates, which have been endorsed by[5] the bank officer, along with the transfer fee. Please include a letter of instruction. Mail these materials[6] to my attention at Investors Exchange at 300 Washington Boulevard. Please send this by registered[7] mail. New securities will be returned to you within two weeks.

If you encounter any difficulties, please[8] call me personally. Very truly yours, (168)

3

Dear Ms. Hatfield:

Thank you for delivering such an inter-esting and informative speech. I could easily[1] see that the other investors enjoyed your remarks as much as I did. As usual, your ideas were[2] stimulating and refreshing. It is easy to see why so many people enjoy hearing you talk.

The[3] audience listened carefully to your advice. You presented some excellent suggestions on how to conduct[4] audits. Many of us leave such matters to our accounting departments, but it is time we accepted certain[5] aspects of that responsibility for ourselves.

I saw many people taking notes during the evening. I am[6] sure that the sales of your new book will reflect the success of your ideas. You have our sincere thanks for a speech that[7] was timely and useful. I hope you will be able to join us again next year. Yours truly, (156)

4

Dear Dr. Gray:

We are very interested in the course you are offering at Westport Junior College.[1] According to the advertisement in the newspaper, the subject of the course will be legal guidelines for[2] investments and securities. Because several laws have been passed recently, this course appears to meet a real need[3] in our community.

We have a large staff who would benefit from such a course, and I am writing to ask if you[4] could accommodate up to 20 people. It is our policy to reimburse employees for all expenses[5] connected with college courses that are successfully completed. Therefore, we would expect most employees[6] to take advantage of this opportunity.

If you find that you cannot enroll all of our employees in[7] the class, would you consider opening a second class? I would be glad to meet with you any time to discuss[8] this exciting possibility. Very truly yours, (170)

5

Dear Miss Little:

Thank you for your letter of March 1. Here is the listing of mutual funds that you requested.[1] As you can see from this brief history, the return has varied a great deal over the years. This year's top fund may[2] be producing the highest earnings now, but we cannot predict how it will compare with other funds next year.[3]

How do you choose among these funds? It is important to remember that you are not restricted to any plan.[4] You can always move your money when market conditions change.

Having reviewed your current status, I recommend[5] that you neither increase nor decrease the shares that you presently hold in mutual funds. Since you are very[6] interested in investing additional money, I would like to suggest some alternatives that might add[7] greater balance to your overall plan.

Why don't you stop by one day this week and look at some other options? Yours[8] truly, (161)

LESSON

29

1

Dear Mr. Roberts:

Thank you for your letter requesting information about retirement plans. The enclosed[1] brochure describes some of the many options available to you.

It is unfortunate for people to become[2] committed to one investment plan. If you are to have financial security during your retirement, you[3] need to have several avenues of income.

We would be happy to invest your funds in any number of[4] stocks, certificates, treasury bills, and mutual funds. Once we have your approval, we can switch your funds from one[5] investment to another to obtain the best yield for you.

I recommend that we sit down and explore these[6] ideas together. There are many ways to make your money work for you. Sincerely yours, (136)

2

Dear Miss Trent:

You are quite right to be concerned about investing in firms that are located in foreign countries.[1] Although many investments are safe, there are always risks. The host government may prove to be unstable, and the[2] exchange rate is constantly subject to change.

Because it is difficult to measure the amount of risk involved,[3] we have taken extra steps to protect our clients. We have developed a staff of 50 trained specialists to keep[4] you advised about foreign markets. They know when it is possible to make the greatest gain for the least amount[5] of risk, and they know when to withdraw your funds altogether.

It would be our pleasure to assist you in making[6] your decisions. Call our office and ask for me. As the director of our international division,[7] I will be glad to help. Cordially yours, (147)

3

Dear Mr. Marshall:

We are pleased to welcome you as a new stockholder of American Electronics. The[1] annual meeting of stockholders will be held at the Royal Hotel in Denver on May 7. Lunch will be[2] served at 12:30, and a review of the year's activities will begin promptly at 1 o'clock.

Toward the[3] end of this meeting, five new directors will be elected. Nominations are expected to be made from the[4] floor, and a vote will be taken subsequently.

If you plan to attend the meeting, please make a reservation[5] according to the regulations shown on the attached page. If we do not receive voting instructions from you,[6] your absence will be considered as a vote for the adoption of all proposals in agreement with company[7] management.

The enclosed report explains the issues to be discussed at the annual meeting. We urge you[8] to join us in planning for the future. Very truly yours, (171)

4

Dear Mr. Sanders:

I would like to recommend a financial advisor for your firm. Ms. Janet Lee has worked[1] with us for more than four years. I can assure you that her knowledge is current, thorough, and reliable.

She has[2] earned the respect of her clients. Many of them have commented that she researches opportunities very[3] thoroughly before recommending them to her clients. They also report that she is attentive to all of[4] her accounts. Even on very short notice, she is usually accessible to everyone she serves.

It[5] has been a pleasure to have her work for us. We will miss her cheerful disposition as well as her professional[6] knowledge of market conditions.

If you feel that you need greater assurance regarding her qualifications,[7] please talk with me personally. Yours truly, (149)

5

Dear Mr. Henderson:

Thank you for your letter regarding your former employee, Sue Carson. I am delighted[1] to say that she has been working with us for nearly six weeks. Even in this short period of time, she has[2] already brought several new clients to our firm.

She mentioned that you helped to form a foundation that has had[3] a positive effect on economic development in your community. This sounds like the kind of[4] program that would greatly benefit our town. Could you share some of your insights into getting such a program started?[5] We have a great deal of support among the leaders in our community, but we need to direct more energy[6] toward economic planning. Having learned of your work, I believe that we could accomplish this much faster[7] with your help.

I will be attending a convention in your city next month. I would appreciate meeting with[8] you then. Yours very truly, (165)

LESSON
30

1

Dear Mr. Kelly:

Congratulations upon your retirement. You must feel very proud of having served in the[1] federal government for nearly three decades.

You have another reason to feel happy. Because you made an[2] important decision long ago to protect your future, you can now enjoy the rewards. You and your wife can[3] look forward to as much prosperity after retirement as you enjoyed during those years as a public servant.[4]

I have enclosed a summary of your current investments. Most of your earnings are from stocks that have shown a[5] steady growth over a long period. We commend your judgment.

Now that your lifestyle is changing, you may wish to[6] make changes in your portfolio. You may wish to convert some real estate into liquid assets. I can[7] recommend some options that will yield greater profits in a shorter period of time.

Please notify me when[8] you are ready to discuss this matter. Yours truly, (169)

2

Dear Mr. and Mrs. Chester:

We would like to remind you that your dividends will grow even more if you[1] reinvest. There are several opportunities that might be of interest to you. The bond market is[2] particularly strong right now. The yield on utilities is expected to rise within the year. We have seen an[3] ongoing interest in the transportation industry, which is expected to continue its growth throughout this[4] decade.

When we talked the last time, you mentioned that you would like to know about special opportunities on the[5] local level. If you are still interested, there are some recent developments that I would like to tell you[6] about.

I can be reached daily at the number listed in the above letterhead. Talking with you is always[7] an enjoyable experience, and I would welcome the opportunity to do it more often. Yours very[8] truly, (162)

3

Dear Sir or Madam:

We have designed a fund that will preserve the capital that you have worked hard to earn. If[1] you are looking for a safe way to watch your cash grow, consider the Corporate Income Fund. At the same time that[2] it is protecting your money, this fund allows you to have immediate access to your account. Yet, it does so[3] without charging a commission fee or an interest penalty.

How can we offer you so much while charging[4] you so little? The answer is simple. You have the benefit of using your own knowledge of the market to[5] oversee your investments. By providing your own evaluations and making your own decisions, you are[6] converting your knowledge into cash.

The Corporate Income Fund offers exciting opportunities to[7] anyone having a knowledge of investments. You provide the direction, and we handle the paperwork.

Look[8] into this matter today. Very truly yours, (168)

4

Gentlemen:

As occupants of a professional office, you see many clients each day. Have you considered[1] subscribing to the leading business journal?

View from Wall Street, America's successful business publication,[2] far outsold its competition last year. To help you see why, we have included a sample copy with this letter.[3] Read it and tell us what you think.

If you would like to receive our journal monthly, just return the enclosed card.[4] We will enroll you as a guest subscriber, and you will receive the first three issues absolutely free.

Take a[5] few minutes now to compare our news and format with other publications you have seen. The depth and range of[6] coverage are helpful to any serious businessperson. Our purpose is to provide a regular survey[7] of the world of business and finance.

Be our guest. Subscribe now and receive three issues free of charge. Cordially yours,[8] (160)

5

Dear Ms. Henry:

A few weeks ago I received a letter from you in which you referred to several investment[1] plans. I will soon be receiving a large amount of cash from my retirement account, and my wife and I have[2] decided to investigate opportunities for investing most of these funds. In order to make these[3] decisions, we both feel that we need the advice of a stock broker.

In addition to this cash settlement, we[4] also have accumulated a large sum in government bonds. We have been thinking of converting these into[5] cash in order to purchase stock. If we were to do so, would we be risking our securities by seeking a[6] higher yield? Would you be able to make this transition for us?

There are several things we would like to discuss[7] with you before reaching a decision. I would appreciate it if you could arrange to meet with us. Sincerely,[8] (160)

LESSON

31

1

Dear Dr. Winters:

Here are the brochures you requested. Please note that hotel rates and air fares are always subject[1] to change. However, the rates listed in these materials will give you a general idea of what to[2] expect.

If this is your first trip abroad, you might wish to consider traveling with a tour group. There are many[3] charter trips available. They usually offer discounted prices, and they provide you with an experienced[4] tour leader.

When you are ready to discuss specific places and dates, our agency will be happy to[5] serve you. We can help you plan a trip that is convenient, fun, and affordable.

I am attaching my business[6] card. Please put it in a handy place so that you can refer to it when needed. Sincerely yours, (138)

2

Dear Ms. Donaldson:

Congratulations on being named saleswoman of the year. You must feel very proud and[1] excited to receive this honor.

As the winner of this contest, you will receive a one-week vacation in[2] Mexico City for you and your husband. Our travel agency has been asked to make all of the necessary[3] arrangements at no charge to you. Your first-place award will pay all expenses for air fares, hotel accommodations,[4] and transportation to and from the airport.

In addition, you will receive $300 in spending[5] money, $500 for meals, and $200 for miscellaneous expenses—sightseeing trips,[6] tips, etc. If you would like to take a driving tour, a rental car will be made available to you[7] at a discounted rate.

You may make your reservations for any week between the dates of May 15 and[8] December 15. We advise you to do this early in order to get your choice of dates. Very truly yours,[9] (180)

3

Dear Mr. and Mrs. Anderson:

Thank you for writing to tell us about your experiences in London.[1] It is very important for us to know about the uncomfortable conditions you described. We have stayed[2] in that hotel on various occasions and have found it to be excellent in every way. However, the[3] hotel has changed hands recently. We will certainly evaluate the new management before recommending[4] these accommodations to other clients.

We are sorry that you found this hotel to be unsatisfactory.[5] We hope that this disappointing experience did not affect the rest of your trip. Thank you again for alerting[6] us, and we would appreciate it if you would keep us informed about other travel experiences.[7] Yours very truly, (144)

4

Dear Mrs. Williams:

Yes, we do offer a discount of 10 percent for groups of 30 or more people. If you[1] would like to make reservations for a three-hour cruise to any of the surrounding islands, you must submit your[2] request 60 days in advance.

The regular prices of tickets range from $42.50 to[3] $70. The exact price depends upon the time of the cruise as well as the destination. Meals, snacks,[4] and drinks are additional and are not included in this price.

Our fleet of ships, the largest of its kind, offers[5] a wide range of schedules. We have many of the same accommodations that larger ocean liners offer. Your[6] trip will be comfortable, relaxing, and thoroughly enjoyable.

I am including additional[7] literature for your inspection. As soon as you have decided upon a date, I will be happy to complete[8] the arrangements. Yours truly, (165)

5

Dear Mrs. Hudson:

Thank you for your letter requesting information regarding our campsites. The enclosed pamphlets[1] will tell you about our facilities, our seasonal rates, and the activities we sponsor for children.[2] I have also included some brochures showing local areas of interest that are within easy driving[3] distance of our camp.

Provisions at each site include electricity, water, and picnic tables. Motor[4] homes and travel trailers of all sizes are welcome. We also have reserved six acres for camping with tents.[5] It is a beautiful wooded area that is perfect for hiking and nature study.

Since our property[6] joins the state park, many of our campers enjoy the activities offered there in addition to those we offer.[7] As a matter of precaution, we suggest that you make reservations in advance.

Thank you again for your[8] interest. Cordially yours, (164)

LESSON

32

1

Dear Miss Conrad:

As your new travel agent, I want you to have confidence in the arrangements I make for you.[1] Therefore, when major changes have to be made in your travel plans, here is the way I will handle them.

As soon as[2] I become aware that adjustments are necessary, I will notify you immediately. To ensure[3] that your arrangements are free of problems, I will call the transportation agent and the hotel desk to confirm[4] the reservations.

I will also forward information on price changes and alterations in transporation[5] routes. Although we give you the most reliable arrangements possible, changes do occur from time to time.[6] I will do all I can to make your trip pleasant for you. Cordially, (132)

2

Dear Ms. Madison:

I will retire from my current position as personnel director in six months. My wife[1] and I are looking forward to celebrating this occasion by taking a vacation somewhere very special.[2]

Since we have never been out of this country, we are considering taking a long trip either to Africa[3] or Japan. What information do you have on these countries? We prefer not to stay in hotels that are[4] elaborate and expensive, but we do want to have accommodations that are safe, comfortable, and[5] easily accessible to transportation.

We have also talked about visiting Western Europe. We would[6] especially like to visit Rome, Italy, and Madrid, Spain.

Your travel agency has always been a great help[7] to my company. I am now looking forward to working with you personally. Sincerely, (156)

3

Dear Miss Baker:

Enclosed is a brochure from the Re-gency Hotel. We have made your reservation for the dates[1] you requested. We certainly hope that you enjoy your stay.

As I explained by phone yesterday, this is one of the[2] most popular hotels among businesspersons. It is conveniently located in the heart of the business[3] district. Yet, it is an old and elegant structure with a great deal of history associated with it.[4] It is charming and comfortable.

I am also including a guide to restaurants and entertainment.[5] You will find many delightful choices for dining while you are there, but I have circled a few that have been[6] recommended by other travelers. I understand that the dinner theater near your hotel is a[7] favorite attraction. Perhaps you will want to plan your evenings as soon as you arrive.

Your airplane ticket will be[8] coming in a few days. Thank you for allowing us to help. Yours very truly, (174)

4

Dear Mr. Hardy:

We received your request for an address change. We will be happy to mail your copy of the[1] newspaper to your temporary address at 118 West Elm Street in Tampa, Florida, during the winter[2] months. It will not be necessary to alter your subscription rate. We charge the same rate for mail delivery[3] as we charge for home delivery.

Please sign the enclosed card. Be sure to specify exact dates for stopping[4] home delivery in January and resuming it in the spring. If you know of friends like yourself who would[5] enjoy reading about home-town news, please pass the word to them that their subscriptions can be transferred easily.[6] Some people simply cancel their subscription for the winter months because they don't realize that they can have the[7] newspaper mailed to them at no additional charge.

Have a great time while you are away. Yours truly, (157)

5

Dear Sir:

I am writing to inquire about the use of your resort for a retreat that we are planning for our[1] sales staff.

The event is tentatively scheduled to be held sometime during the month of September. It is to[2] last a week, and we will need accommodations for approximately 25 people.

Please let me know what[3] you have to offer in facilities. For every day of our stay, we will need a large meeting room that will[4] accommodate a movie projector and screen. We would also like to know what is available in recreation.[5] We are interested in tennis, swimming, golf, etc. Is it possible to rent boats for use in the[6] lake near your hotel?

Please include information on discounts that you offer to groups or corporations. If[7] your facilities are appropriate for our purpose, I will call you soon to choose a week during September.[8] Very truly yours, (164)

LESSON

33

1

Dear Mr. Leonard:

We are delighted to assist you in planning your family vacation. Over the years[1] we have learned that the best vacations are planned ahead. You have already learned that taking chances on finding[2] accommodations far from home can lead to discomfort and expense.

In the packet that we have enclosed, you will find[3] information on airline rates and schedules, hotels, and guided tours. As you requested, we emphasized places[4] in the northeastern United States. If you would still like to consider a southwestern route after showing these[5] materials to your family, I will mail additional literature to you immediately.

In[6] order to ensure that you get your choice of lodging and transportation, we should book your reservations at least[7] three months in advance. The tourist season is expected to begin early this year.

When the time for your vacation[8] arrives, your arrangements will be all ready for you. We are always eager to be of assistance. Very[9] truly yours, (182)

2

Dear Mr. Carson:

Please reserve a double room for me for November 5 through November 13. My wife and[1] I will arrive in the early afternoon after a lengthy trip from California. We will fly out of[2] San Francisco on Flight No. 217. It will arrive in New Haven at 1:05 p.m. Eastern[3] Standard Time. Please make certain that the hotel room is ready for us by 2 p.m.

I will also need a[4] conference room for the morning of November 7. The room should be large enough to seat about 15 people[5] comfortably. We will need a large table and a slide projector and screen. I will be ordering breakfast to be[6] served at 8:30 that morning.

Please send confirmation of these arrangements right away. I understand that there[7] will be a large convention in town that week, and I wish to be certain that adequate accommodations will[8] be available for us.

Thank you very much for overseeing this matter. Cordially, (176)

3

Dear Mrs. Mason:

Thank you for your interest in Happy Valley Ranch. We hope the enclosed booklet answers your[1] questions.

As you can see, every day at our ranch is a long and fun-filled occasion. You can join a trail ride[2] into the mountains to see the sun come up, and you can cook fresh beef over an open fire when the sun goes down.[3] We have heard it said by people down here that they can smell that good western cooking for miles around.

Those who don't like[4] horseback riding can enjoy swimming, tennis, a health club, and much more. Little wranglers under the age of five are[5] under the care of a qualified trail boss.

Mrs. Mason, we are glad that you are thinking about being with us[6] during your vacation. We look forward to your visit. Yours very truly, (134)

4

Dear Frank:

Here are the pamphlets you requested about camping locations. I am also including a guide to[1] the state parks, which I think you will find informative.

There are some beautiful campsites located within easy[2] driving distance from your home. Within a radius of 150 miles, there are four state parks with excellent[3] camping facilities.

If you would like to know more about cabins, I am including a list of private[4] and public resorts that offer cabins for rent. The enclosed rate sheet may be slightly out of date, but it will give[5] you an idea of how the different places compare with each other. Most campsites have increased their prices[6] by approximately 5 percent since last year.

There is one other possibility you may wish to consider.[7] Some of our state parks have lodges and inns that have a rich, rustic charm. When compared to other hotels, the prices[8] are especially reasonable. Sincerely yours, (170)

5

Dear Mrs. Middleton:

I understand that your committee will choose the site for the next annual merchandising[1] convention. May I offer a suggestion?

Please take a good look at Austin, Texas. Many people already[2] know that we are the home of a great university. How many people realize, however, that we[3] also offer a fine convention center that can easily accommodate your registered guests?

Our convention[4] complex is located in the heart of downtown. You will have easy access to shopping, eating establishments,[5] and theaters. The center is only 15 minutes from the main campus of one of our state's largest[6] universities.

We are certain that our rates will be very attractive to your committee. When you compare them[7] to alternative sites in larger cities, we believe that you will be favorably impressed with what we have[8] to offer. Respectfully yours, (166)

LESSON
34

1

Dear Mr. and Mrs. Hunter:

This letter will confirm your reservations at our beautiful hotel. You will[1] have a room here beginning on August 8, and your reservations will continue through August 22. As[2] you requested, the room will have a view of the ocean.

I realize that these dates are one week later than you[3] wanted originally. As I recall, August 1 was your first choice. I can still make your reservation for[4] that date, but you will not have a seaside room. If you want me to make this change, please let me know immediately.[5]

The room rate is well within the price range you specified. I am sure that you will be pleased with the accommodations,[6] our courteous service, and our dining room that overlooks the bay.

Please let me know if you wish to make[7] additional arrangements for a rental car. I will be happy to put such a plan into motion for you.[8]

We look forward to having you as our guests. Very truly yours, (171)

2

Dear Friends:

Here is a wonderful idea for a Christmas present. Why not give the gift of travel?

Air Travel[1] Club is making a special offer as part of a membership drive. You can now purchase a family membership[2] for as little as $100. You pay only the initial fee for joining. Once you are a member,[3] you pay a minimal monthly charge to cover administrative costs.

We sponsor two weekend trips per month.[4] In addition, we have regular flights to major cities. Some typical examples are Miami, Atlanta,[5] New York, Detroit, and Los Angeles. For a relatively low cost, you can fly from state to state. Visit[6] Florida, Virginia, New York, and Maine for prices you never dreamed possible.

Yet, you are not confined to the[7] United States. We plan six trips abroad each year. Expand your horizon. Call today. Sincerely yours, (157)

3

Dear Mrs. Phillips:

Enclosed is a certificate that entitles you to a discount on your next trip with[1] Eagle Airlines. We apologize for the inconvenience caused you by the recent misunderstanding. Although we[2] try to be very accurate in booking flights, mistakes do happen from time to time. When a situation like[3] yours develops, we do all we can to minimize your discomfort and get you to your destination as quickly[4] as possible.

In your case, Mrs. Phillips, even though we could not get you on board your regularly scheduled[5] flight with us, we did make the arrangements to seat you on a plane with another airline. It is our usual[6] policy to cooperate with our neighbors when it means giving better service to our customers.

When[7] you book your next flight, please notify the reservation desk that you will be applying the courtesy coupon.[8] We thank you for your patience in this matter. Yours very truly, (171)

4

Dear Miss Ray:

We have prepared the enclosed itinerary for your trip to Japan. If you approve of these[1] arrangements, we will make your reservations at once.

We are enclosing information to answer your questions[2] about preparing for the trip. As explained in the government handbook, you will need a visa in addition[3] to your passport. If you have not already done so, please take your birth certificate and two black-and-white photographs[4] to the post office. There will be a modest fee, and your passport will be mailed to you within a few weeks.

I[5] understand that you will be visiting this distant country when it is particularly festive. If you have[6] any more questions, don't hesitate to ask. Please let me know immediately if the arrangements look okay[7] to you. Yours truly, (143)

5

Dear Professor Egan:

Here is the information you requested about academic tours abroad. As you[1] can see, we have established programs in several countries. You can spend two weeks in one of these locations, where[2] you will study a variety of subjects related to history and literature. Classes will also[3] be taught in politics, drama, and art.

Our prices include your room, tuition, and a portion of your meals.[4] You will find yourself among friends who share your interests. If you are like most people who enroll in our academic[5] tours, you will make lifetime friends during this period.

Since we must limit the number of applications that[6] we can accept, we encourage you to make your reservation early. We look forward to aiding you in[7] this exciting experience. Cordially yours, (149)

LESSON

35

1

Dear Ms. Mitchell:

This is in response to your recent letter concerning the loss of items. After checking your[1] room, we did discover that you had left a book and a briefcase. We are storing these items in a safe place[2] located behind our front desk.

If you would like to have these items shipped or mailed to you, please instruct us on the[3] method of delivery. If you would like to have a friend pick them up at the front desk for you, please notify us[4] of your intention. We will gladly present the items if we know whom to expect and if the person presents[5] proper identification.

We are sorry that you have been inconvenienced by this problem, and we will[6] gladly help all we can to find a remedy. Sincerely yours, (131)

2

Dear Mr. and Mrs. Carlson:

We wanted you to know about a special family plan we are offering[1] this summer. Since you have vacationed with us in the past, you should know that we are introducing a new efficiency[2] rate for families of four or more people.

To qualify for this rate, you must stay a minimum of[3] 14 days. During this time you will have the use of a furnished apartment complete with kitchen, dining table[4] and chairs, living room with sofa bed, and bedroom with two double beds. Laundry facilities are located[5] within walking distance of each apartment.

If you are interested in getting the most economical[6] rate possible, we can place you in a nice, comfortable apartment located about 100 yards from[7] the ocean.

Make your plans now and enjoy the islands during the months of June, July, and August. The sun and fun[8] await you at bargain prices. Cordially yours, (168)

3

Dear Mr. Christopher:

Emerald Airlines will be pleased to welcome you aboard our holiday flight No.[1] 336. It departs from the international airport on December 20 for Miami.

We notice[2] that you did not take advantage of the side trip that we have arranged. As part of your flight plan, you are eligible[3] to take a one-day trip to the islands at half the regular fare. This is the fly-sail package that has gained[4] us so much national attention. It has been very successful in the past, and many customers tell us[5] that the cruise is the highlight of their trip.

If you wish to be registered for the cruise, please return the enclosed[6] reservation. The tickets will be held for you at our flight reservation desk.

Thank you for flying Emerald.[7] Sincerely yours, (143)

4

Dear Class Member:

We are happy to announce that charter flights are being arranged for the summer. As a senior[1] at New Haven College, you qualify for special round-trip fares and discount rates at many hotels. Flights have been[2] scheduled to arrive in Rome, London, and Athens. These charter flights are of varying duration and cost.

Charter[3] flights offer educational opportunities to students at exceptionally low prices. If you place[4] your reservation before March 7, you will be entitled to an additional discount of $50.[5] To make your reservation, include a deposit of $200. Deposits are returnable[6] up to 30 days prior to departure.

There are only a limited number of seats available on[7] all flights. Plan now to go abroad with friends and colleagues. We don't want to leave home without you. Very truly yours,[8] (160)

5

Dear Mr. Vernon:

I am in the process of writing a book about your beautiful state. On several[1] occasions during the past ten years, I have enjoyed many vacations there. I have climbed your mountains, camped in your woods,[2] and fished in your famous rivers. I have often watched the sun set over those blue, shining waters.

I have also[3] shopped in your small towns and dined in your busy cities. I have taken photographs from every angle. I can show[4] you pictures that were taken from a boat, from an airplane, and even from a mining car.

I have become friends with[5] your residents, and I have grown to love their customs. I have recorded most of what I have observed in photographs.[6]

I know that your company publishes textbooks and journals. Would you consider looking at a truly[7] exceptional story about your state? I will gladly forward a sample of my work to you. Yours very truly,[8] (160)

LESSON

36

1

Dear Miss Martin:

Thank you for your inquiry about purchasing advertising space in our magazine. Our readers[1] are very interested in home decorating, and your products will have excellent exposure in our[2] magazine regardless of where we place your ad. However, I am recommending that we choose a special section[3] devoted to arts and crafts. Since your products are fabrics, they are certain to attract attention there.

I am[4] enclosing a rate card for your information. As you can see, there is an additional charge required for placing[5] your ad in a specific section. If you feel that the readership is much better for that section, the placement[6] fee is nominal in comparison to the increase in sales that will result.

Please notice that the most expensive[7] ad is the one that runs one time only. The most economical plan available is our annual[8] contract plan. We encourage you to give it careful consideration.

Please let us know what you have decided.[9] Very truly yours, (184)

2

Dear Mr. Edwards:

I want to welcome you as a new advertiser. Also, I have been asked to help plan your[1] advertising schedule as soon as possible.

You are now running 15 commercials a week, and all of these[2] are aired during prime time in the early morning or in the late afternoon. I would like for you to think about[3] scheduling some additional announcements during the middle of the day. I am sure that you are familiar[4] with our morning talk show, for example. This popular program, which is hosted by J. J. Nelson, comes on the[5] air at 10 o'clock Monday through Friday. It is noted for its success in selling household products, and I think[6] you would get excellent results from your commercials.

Our noonday report is another show which has a large[7] listening audience. I understand that you are coming into our station next week. I look forward to getting[8] together with you to make our plans. Yours truly, (169)

3

Dear Mr. Gregory:

I will be delighted to join the staff of your advertising agency. I am pleased[1] that you have extended the invitation, and I will do everything I can to justify the confidence[2] you have shown in me.

As I explained by phone yesterday, I do have a very important campaign underway[3] in my current position. Although I am eager to assume my new duties with your firm, I feel that I must[4] complete my responsibilities here before I leave this job. Therefore, I cannot be available on the[5] date you specified.

Perhaps we can find a solution to the problem. My employer may be willing to give[6] me a few days off next month to attend your training sessions. That would give me the opportunity to meet your[7] clients and attend the meetings that you have scheduled. I would then return to my current position and complete[8] the project, which would require about two weeks.

I am excited about working for your agency. I hope that[9] this plan is acceptable to you. Yours very truly, (190)

4

Gentlemen:

Do you now own the latest, most effective equipment for showing audio-visual materials?[1] Are your sales presentations limited by your equipment?

You cannot do justice to beautiful slides if[2] your projector breaks down in the middle of a demonstration. A video tape is not going to be[3] effective if the quality of the color is poor or if the pictures are not sharp. If you were to see a[4] demonstration of our products, you would see what a difference fine quality would make. Equipment manufactured[5] by Brown, Inc., is the most sophisticated on the market.

To prove this point, we would like to[6] arrange a special viewing for you. We invite you to bring the best work that your art department has produced. If[7] you don't agree that our equipment appears to improve the quality of your artwork, we will loan you the use[8] of our equipment for one month free of charge.

Take an important step toward success. Call us today. Cordially[9] yours, (181)

5

Dear Joyce:

I am concerned about the Christmas commercials that your agency is producing for our firm. I can't[1] help wondering if they are becoming out of date. I believe we should make some changes that would enable us[2] to use our commercials during the Christmas season for several years to come.

For example, the gowns and hair[3] styles currently being used are representative of high fashion. If we were to substitute attractive,[4] traditional hair styles and conservative styles of clothing, our commercials would have a classic appeal. We could use[5] them for many years.

Please don't think that I am unhappy with the quality of work you are giving us. Your[6] agency is creative and very professional. I have a great deal of respect for your ideas, and[7] I know that I can count on your advice.

Please think about this matter and get back to me. Sincerely yours, (158)

LESSON
37

1

MEMO TO: All Staff Members

Congratulations on a job well done. I am referring, of course, to the fact that[1] we have just won our first national advertising award. What an honor this is for everyone in this[2] department!

It is impossible to point to a single person who is responsible for this successful[3] effort. Everyone contributed to the excellence of our fall campaign. The awards committee has stated[4] that our campaign was outstanding. Furthermore, we have been commended for demonstrating high ethical values.[5] We are proud and pleased to have chosen a campaign that was associated with the historical background of[6] this city.

We invite you to attend the awards ceremony on May 7. The publisher of the[7] newspaper will be on hand to help present the award to our department store. In addition, the mayor will[8] address our group.

We hope that each of you will be present. (169)

2

Dear Patricia:

I am writing this letter to confirm that we have rescheduled the commercial announcement that[1] was supposed to be shown on September 3. Because of a special address by the President, we were unable[2] to air your 30-second spot as scheduled at 7:13 p.m.

We will make up that time by running[3] your announcement during the evening newscast on September 9. This is an excellent program, and it has a[4] very high viewing audience. I feel certain that you will be pleased with the television exposure you will[5] receive.

I hope this arrangement will be satisfactory. It was a pleasure talking with you yesterday, and[6] I look forward to seeing you again soon. As always, I am available to meet with you any time to[7] review your advertising goals. Sincerely, (148)

3

Dear Sir or Madam:

Are you well informed about what is happening in the business world? If you read *Advertising*[1] *Review* each week, you can be confident that your knowledge is accurate and up to date.

Time is a valuable[2] asset for the professional. That is why we employ a staff of writers and researchers to find the news[3] for you. They sort through the week's happenings and present the most significant information in a format[4] that is convenient for you to read. You can easily locate the articles that are most important to you.[5] At the same time, however, you can see what is happening elsewhere without reading long, complicated stories.[6]

To show you what we mean, we are making this trial offer. If you subscribe for four months, we will send the first four[7] issues to you free of charge.

Complete the enclosed card today. For only a nominal investment, you will[8] receive a million dollars worth of solid information. Very truly yours, (174)

4

MEMO TO: Pamela Stevens

I have just come from a meeting with your newest client, York Industries. As I had[1] expected, they were extremely pleased with the presentation you made last week. They are excited about the[2] plans you outlined for their account, and they would like for you to continue in that same direction.

The advertising[3] manager stressed that they wish to preserve the image that they have established. Their advertisements should reflect[4] stability and quality of service. Since you have had a great deal of experience with this kind of account,[5] I do not anticipate that you will have any problems.

If you still want to review the budget for this[6] account, I will be happy to look at your suggestions. It is now up to you to show that we can deliver[7] the kind of campaign that we have promised. Call on me if I can be of assistance. (155)

5

MEMO TO: Ed Foster

I am attaching copies of invoices for recent promotions that we have sponsored.[1] Let me explain why the actual costs are higher than we had estimated.

When we made our original[2] plans, we decided to advertise in four trade journals. We scheduled those ads accordingly. We were subsequently[3] offered an unusual opportunity to advertise in two national magazines. Each has an[4] excellent market penetration.

Although the costs of these two ads may appear to be high at first glance, they are[5] actually discount rates. We felt that it was fortunate for us to get the national exposure at the[6] quoted prices.

I appreciate your concern about the budget, but I believe that the benefit will far[7] exceed the cost. We are delighted with the responses that we are already receiving from the national[8] ads.

I hope that my explanation has answered your questions, Ed. (171)

LESSON

38

1

Dear Mr. Webster:

Thank you for your brochure about the role of advertising in our economy. In a[1] system of free enterprise, advertising helps to educate the consumer. Many buyers depend upon[2] advertisements to tell them everything they want to know about the products they wish to purchase.

Our school is[3] sponsoring an introduction to careers next month, and advertising is among the areas to be[4] presented. Could you send us 200 copies of your brochure?

If you can, please send the brochures to me at the[5] address given above. Please include a bill for the mailing fees as well as for the materials. I hope you can[6] meet our deadline of November 12. If you cannot, would you please let me know?

We certainly will be able to make[7] good use of your materials. Cordially yours, (149)

2

Dear Reader:

There is a surprise in store for you. Something new will arrive at your door next week, and we would like you[1] to accept it as a gift from us. It is the *Wall Street Post*, the publication used by financial experts across[2] the nation.

Why is the *Post* so popular? First of all, it is written by several leading authorities.[3] Second, it contains up-to-date information. Third, it is reliable.

There are many more reasons, but[4] we are inviting you to form your own opinion. Spend some time reading this interesting publication. It[5] will bring you closer to the political and financial developments that shape our economy.

If you[6] like what you see, you may subscribe on a trial basis at a special discount rate. We think you will become one[7] of the thousands of business people around the country who start their day with a cup of coffee and a copy[8] of the *Post*. Yours very truly, (166)

3

Dear Ms. Trent:

A few weeks ago we sent a rate card to

you at your request. At that time you were thinking of[1] purchasing advertising space in a magazine for professional women.

Ms. Trent, we are delighted that[2] you are considering our publication. We think that you should know about a special edition that we are[3] planning for December. This particular issue will carry the top news stories of this year. It will include[4] interviews with leading businesswomen in the country, and it will discuss other topics of interest to[5] women.

This issue seems to be particularly appropriate for you. I am enclosing another rate card[6] for your convenience. If you decide to purchase space, please make your reservation right away. This is a popular[7] issue, and we anticipate receiving a large response.

Thank you again for your interest. Respectfully[8] yours, (161)

4

Dear Mr. Rogers:

After our interview last Wednesday, I gave much consideration to the kind of advertising[1] your company needs. I believe that your ads should reflect your success on the international scene. We could[2] accomplish this by making films and photographs in foreign locations. We would want to emphasize the excellent[3] relations you are experiencing with the host countries.

The drama of these international settings[4] would attract attention. In these new television commercials, we would use the script to reinforce the goodwill[5] for which your company is known. We would use the same approach in writing the ad copy for the printed media.[6]

Now that I have given more thought to the matter, Mr. Rogers, I am certain that we can produce exactly[7] what you are looking for. Would you be available sometime to look at some rough sketches? Very truly yours,[8] (160)

5

Dear Mrs. Donaldson:

I was pleased to learn that some of your students wish to choose careers in advertising.[1] We are always looking for talented people who have the ability to communicate ideas. I hope[2] the enclosed literature, which is a recent publication of our agency, will be of use to your class.[3]

Please tell your students that advertising agencies need skilled, dedicated people. We need people with skills in[4] accounting, writing, selling, and researching. Photographers and artists are also very much in demand.[5]

The work pace is fast in an advertising department. The work is often fun, and it is always interesting.[6] According to most of the veterans in this business, it is fascinating work for people who are willing[7] to work hard.

I wish all of your students the best of luck. Cordially yours, (153)

LESSON

39

1

Dear Richard:

We have completed the research on household cleaners that we have been conducting for your firm. I am[1] enclosing a copy of the questionnaire and a copy of the survey results.

As you can see from the data,[2] the majority of the people surveyed responded to your product in a positive manner. More than[3] 60 percent said that they would pay the asking price. While almost 20 percent said that they liked the product and[4] found it to be effective, they thought the suggested retail price was too high. Only 15 percent said that they[5] would not buy the item regardless of price.

This survey was based on a random sample of the population[6] in this region, and it should be considered a reliable sample.

When you have had a chance to study these[7] results carefully, please give me a call. I will arrange to discuss them with you at length. Sincerely, (158)

2

Dear Mrs. Jackson:

Thank you for your order. As you requested, we have reserved space for a full-color ad. It[1] will be four columns wide by 30 inches deep, and it will be positioned in the sports pages.

If you would like[2] to run a follow-up advertisement, we should reserve space for that ad now. Many advertisers choose to use[3] the same artwork and type style used in the original ad. In order to cut costs, however, it is possible[4] to run the second ad in one or two colors. Depending upon the artwork itself, it may be possible[5] to run the second ad in black and white only.

The large, full-color ad is the most expensive option[6] available, and it is often very effective. Sometimes, however, you can achieve the same effectiveness[7] with a follow-up ad of a reduced size. I would suggest that the second ad be three columns wide by[8] 20 inches deep.

Please let me know what you have decided to do. Yours truly, (173)

3

Dear Mr. Davis:

We are interested in having your agency design a sales brochure for us. Although[1] we have experienced steady growth, our objective is to increase sales by 30 percent this year.

As part of[2] this plan, we would like to send brochures to every household in this city and in the five surrounding counties.[3] We are willing to discuss various designs and price ranges. Before making any decisions, we would like[4] to know your standard fees for design, for providing original artwork, and for producing the brochure. It would[5] help us to know the costs of using colored ink, of printing, and of any additional miscellaneous[6] expenses.

I have been impressed with the work of your agency for quite some time. I look forward to hearing from[7] you in regard to this matter. Very truly yours, (149)

4

MEMO TO: Bill Harrison

I would like to compliment you on the ads you are doing for the automobile[1] dealership. I like the general approach you have used.

In looking at the sketches, however, I had some[2] suggestions to pass on to you. Since the owners have specified that they are looking for a contemporary[3] image, I think we should choose new colors. The dark brown and green you have used are attractive, but they do not contribute[4] to a contemporary image. I think they should be changed to bright, bold colors.

I am also concerned about[5] the choice and size of type used for the copy. The type is a heavy style that requires a lot of space. It currently[6] looks crowded on the page. We should either reduce the amount of copy so that less type has to be used, or[7] we should select a different style that would be more appropriate.

I would like to see the sketches again[8] after you have addressed these problems. (166)

5

Dear Mr. Cox:

An electronics firm has contacted us about creating a national campaign for them.[1] The ads would run in major cities across the country. We are excited about this prospect, and we want very[2] much to represent this client. However, we feel we need to have more technical knowledge about the products.[3]

We are aware of the fine work you have done in this area. Would you be free to help us with this particular[4] campaign? The work could be performed on a freelance basis, and you would be paid generously for your time and[5] creative efforts.

You would be working with a support staff of writers, artists, and account supervisors.[6] We would establish deadlines for completing each phase of the campaign.

If you are interested in working on[7] this project, Mr. Cox, please call me no later than Friday of this week. I look forward to hearing from you.[8] Cordially yours, (162)

LESSON
40

1

Dear Mr. Baxter:

I enjoyed meeting you at the luncheon for advertisers. You made a very interest-ing[1] point about the danger of holding too many discount sales. I agree with you that this approach to marketing[2] loses its effectiveness very soon if it is overdone.

It is possible to reduce costs without[3] gaining the reputation of being a discount operation. I am enclosing a brochure which our[4] agency recently designed for a new sporting goods store. The brochure had so much appeal that we were asked to do[5] a similar item for a chain of pharmacies. I think that the general approach could also be used for[6] supermarkets as well as for other types of retail outlets.

We have produced promotion materials for[7] dozens of companies in this region. I would like to show you a sample of our work and discuss ways to[8] apply our approach to your marketing efforts. Cordially yours, (171)

2

Dear Miss Morgan:

Thank you for your inquiry about market research in home furnishings. You are wise to conduct[1] a thorough market analysis. Advertising decisions are often made from habit rather than from[2] careful evaluation. We work with some excellent research firms, and we can certainly arrange to have your[3] questions answered.

Since you plan to sell your line of glassware within a radius of 200 miles, I am[4] recommending the firm of Stanford, Inc. They have completed similar assignments, and their findings[5] have been very reliable. They will obtain the information you need to make decisions about distribution[6] and pricing.

By contacting us, you have taken the first step toward ensuring that your product will command[7] a good share of the market. Why don't you contact my office this week so that we can make plans for the campaign[8] ahead? Yours truly, (164)

3

Dear Mr. Webb:

Thank you for your letter asking about advertising space in our newspaper. A small ad in[1] our classified section would attract many customers to your business. People who read these sections are already[2] looking for your service. Classified ads offer you the most economical way to reach these people.

There[3] are many options available to you. You may place ads on a day-to-day basis, or you may sign a contract[4] for up to a year. There are also two-week arrangements, monthly contracts, and quarterly contracts. The amount[5] you pay per ad depends upon the agreement you have with us. The most economical arrangement, of course,[6] is an annual contract. If you run a minimum of three ads each week for a period of one year, you[7] will receive up to 50 inches of free advertising space.

Thank you again, Mr. Webb, for writing. If you[8] come by my office, we can work out a plan that is effective and economical for you. Our daily[9] circulation is now over 100,000. I know we can help you. Yours very truly, (196)

4

Dear Ms. Howard:

We would be delighted to discuss your advertising plans. We can meet with you during lunch on[1] Monday, January 5, as you suggested. When we meet with you, we will need to have specific information[2] about your products and the emphasis you prefer.

We have contacted a marketing research firm, Midwestern[3] Research, and the executive manager has agreed to give your project priority. I think it is[4] possible to test your new products, conduct a survey, and have the results within six months.

In the meantime,[5] we will begin laying out plans for introducing your product to the public. By the time the test results are in,[6] we will have made the necessary arrangements with the media.

It will be a pleasure to work with you[7] again. Sincerely yours, (144)

5

Dear George:

We are still considering your request to provide materials for the Senator's campaign. As I[1] told you before, I am supportive of your candidate. If we were operating under normal circumstances,[2] we would be delighted to help. However, my staff is concerned that we have already committed ourselves[3] beyond our capacity in this office. We are all feeling the effect of having too much work to do.[4] Because of our current work schedule, we are having to look at your proposal very carefully.

I wonder if[5] we could have two more weeks to consider your project. By the end of that time, we will have completed one major[6] job. We can then review our workload and make a final decision.

I look forward to talking with you then.[7] Sincerely, (142)

LESSON

41

1

Dear Mr. May:

Thank you for your letter inquiring

about a site for your industrial plant. Your letter arrived[1] at an opportune time.

We can suggest two possible sites that might meet your specific needs. Both of these buildings[2] are empty now, and both are available on a rental basis. If you prefer, you may also rent with[3] an option to buy the property. The buildings have housed operations that were similar to yours. They became[4] available when the previous tenants decided to relocate in the South.

Please let me know when you can[5] come to see these buildings, and I will make the arrangements. We believe that our community offers unique[6] advantages for industries like yours. We have an excellent location in the central part of town, and we are[7] situated near a major supplier of machine parts. Yours truly, (153)

2

Dear Mr. Harrison:

I am delighted that you are interested in seeing an apartment located[1] in our finest complex, Twin Towers. I believe that we offer all of the features that you specified in your[2] letter.

Apartments will be ready for occupancy about the time you are planning to move to this city.[3] Our units offer many luxury features in addition to including a beautiful view of the city.[4] We also offer shopping facilities, recreation, and food services. A new sports center is being[5] built next door, which will be connected to our buildings by a private walkway.

Model apartments are now open[6] for your inspection. Call me the next time you are in the city, and I will arrange to show you an apartment.[7] Sincerely yours, (144)

3

Dear Mrs. Ford:

I have several houses to show you when you visit next week. The house that you wanted to[1] inspect on Anderson Street is no longer a possibility; it was sold last week.

However, if you[2] particularly like that neighborhood, I have good news for you. There are several houses currently on the[3] market in that area. I am enclosing some pages from our multiple-listing service. The house on[4] Jefferson Lane would be an excellent buy, for example. It has approximately 2500 square feet[5] of living space which includes a finished basement. The back yard is approximately one-half acre of land.

This[6] subdivision is located in a choice school district. It has an active group of residents, and I think you would[7] enjoy living there. I look forward to seeing you next week. Sincerely yours, (153)

4

Dear Mr. and Mrs. Gregory:

I suggest that we submit an offer for the property in Hidden Valley.[1] You seemed to like that subdivision a great deal, and I would like you to receive your first choice of sites.

Since we[2] last talked, the situation has changed. The sale price has been lowered, and I think that you will be able to buy the[3] property for a very reasonable amount. The current owners contacted me yesterday to see if[4] you were still interested in purchasing the land. They are definitely not interested in building a[5] house on the site, and they would like to reopen negotiations with you.

I would like to have your advice[6] before I talk again with the owners. Please let me know what you wish to do. Cordially, (135)

5

Dear Margaret:

Congratulations on having an outstanding year in sales. It must have been very exciting[1] to learn that you had sold a million dollars in real estate during your first year with this agency. This is a[2] remarkable achievement, and you should feel very proud of your effort.

I am certain that you will set new goals[3] for yourself, and I also know that we can expect them to be as challenging as the one you achieved this year.[4] I wish you the best of luck in your future endeavors. You certainly have earned the success that you are enjoying,[5] Margaret. Furthermore, I am sure that you will earn even more as your career progresses. Sincerely yours,[6] (120)

LESSON

42

1

Dear Mr. Davenport:

I have watched the area near the airport carefully, and I believe that I have[1] located the kind of office building you wish to buy. Although its size is suitable, the building can only be[2] purchased with a contract sale. What do you think of this idea?

The terms are favorable, and you would have a[3] fixed rate of interest. The building meets every requirement stated in your letter. The parking lot is large, and[4] there are several access roads located nearby. It is located in an area that has not yet been[5] incorporated into the city limits.

Would you like to send a representative to see this building?[6] I can put together some estimates of utility costs if you are interested in buying the[7] property. I will be waiting to hear from you. Very truly yours, (151)

2

Dear Mrs. Webster:

I have spoken with James Grant, who owns the warehouse at 23 East 71 Street.[1] He is now considering the offer you made to lease his building. However, the executive vice president[2] of the factory next door has made an offer to buy the building. At the present time, Mr. Grant is[3] undecided about what to do.

Would you be interested in leasing with an option to buy? When you consider[4] that the demand for property is increasing in this area, an option agreement may be the best[5] solution for everyone. If you wish to pursue this plan, please let me know at once. I will stay in touch with Mr.[6] Grant until he has made a decision. In the meantime, I will continue to look for an alternative[7] building for your needs.

I will wait to receive further instructions from you regarding this matter. Cordially yours,[8] (160)

3

Dear Mrs. Johnson:

I hope that you are enjoying your retirement in Orlando, Florida. We would love to[1] have some of your warm weather here right now.

Although the real estate market continues to move slowly, we are showing[2] your home about twice a week. We cannot expect real estate to move quickly right now, so I am not concerned[3] that we still do not have a buyer for your house.

I do have some suggestions that may help speed things up, however.[4] Since you moved, a need for maintenance has become apparent. I am asking for your permission to hire someone[5] to do some work in the house; the yard requires some work as well. A few minor repairs will do wonders for a house[6] that is vacant.

These repairs could be accomplished for a modest charge. Please let me know if it is okay to go[7] ahead with the work. Yours very truly, (147)

4

Dear Mr. and Mrs. Doyle:

After we talked yesterday, I learned of another house that has just become available.[1] Because it sounds like the kind of place that you are looking for, I am hopeful that you will find the time to see[2] it this weekend. The house will not be available for showing until Saturday morning, so I am taking[3] the liberty of making an appointment for 9 a.m.

I know this means that you will have to stay in town[4] an additional night, but I believe that you will want to see this house. It has six bedrooms, a finished basement,[5] and a swimming pool. It is situated on a beautiful lot in a very private area.

Furthermore,[6] it is not far from the price range you have given me. Unless I hear from you, I will assume that you are[7] interested in seeing this house at the time specified. Yours truly, (152)

5

Dear Ms. Hunter:

I am pleased that you are considering the two shopping centers as possible sites for opening[1] a new store. Now that you have had time to think about the two locations, I am writing to see if you have[2] made a decision.

If you still have questions about the space available in either site, I suggest that we[3] visit the facilities once more to discuss the possibility of expansion. Since it is better to[4] have too much space than too little, you are wise to look for a large area.

Although a five-year lease is a[5] standard requirement for either location, we might be able to negotiate a shorter lease. I will be[6] available for consultation on Tuesday, Thursday, or Friday of next week. Please let me know when you are ready[7] to discuss these ideas further. Sincerely yours, (149)

LESSON

43

1

Dear Mr. and Mrs. Scott:

You must be pleased that your offer has been accepted. You are about to become the[1] owners of a new apartment building.

Enclosed is a copy of the contract that you will be asked to sign at[2] the time of closing. If you have any questions about the terms, please call me immediately so that I can[3] answer them before we meet officially.

When you buy property on a contract basis rather than purchase[4] a mortgage from a lending institution, the deed to the property is not recorded until the contract[5] is paid off. However, we can pay a fee and have the contract recorded. The recording process is optional,[6] but I recommend that we have it done. By doing so, we will protect your investment in the property.[7]

I do hope that you are pleased with this purchase. It is valuable property, and it will certainly prove to[8] be an excellent investment for you. Sincerely yours, (170)

2

Dear Mr. Barker:

I certainly understand your desire to postpone the sale of your home. Your circumstances[1] have changed radically, and it would be better for you to stay where you are until you have had time to make your[2] decision.

In the meantime, I will remain alert to potential buyers who have shown an interest in your[3] home. If you decide to take the new job in Detroit, I am confident that your house will sell quickly.

I would[4] also like to remind you that we may be able to assist you in locating a new home in Detroit.[5] We can initiate a computer search for a house with the features that you prefer.

Again, thank you for[6] allowing us to assist you. If I can be of help to you at any time, please call me. Cordially, (138)

3

Dear Dr. and Mrs. Cox:

I am pleased to say that the owners have accepted your offer to purchase the house[1] on Stevenson Street. The earnest money that you submitted has been deposited into an escrow account.[2] At the time of closing, that earnest money will be withdrawn from escrow and applied toward the mortgage that you are[3] purchasing.

I cannot give you an exact date for taking possession of the house, but I will let you know[4] as soon as I have that information. The bank must set a date for the closing, and we expect that date to be[5] five or six weeks away. Between now and the time of closing, I will prepare a list of the procedures that will be[6] necessary to transfer the title. In keeping with your request, I will also give you an itemized list[7] of the fees that will be due at the time of closing.

It has been a joy working with you, and I am delighted[8] that things have gone so well for everyone. Yours truly, (170)

4

Dear Ms. Foster:

When I was driving through your neighborhood this morning, I noticed that your home is for sale by owner.[1] Have you considered the many advantages of listing your house with a realtor?

Although many people[2] attempt to sell their homes by themselves, they often find that there is much more to selling real estate than they had thought.[3] For example, a realtor has many contacts and knows how to reach prospective buyers. Another major[4] consideration is that a realtor is a licensed agent. He or she has a great deal of knowledge[5] about the legal and financial aspects of transferring ownership.

Buying or selling your home is one of[6] the most important investments you will ever make. Why risk this investment by placing that responsibility[7] in the hands of an amateur?

Enclosed is my business card, Ms. Foster. I would be happy to visit your[8] home and give you an appraisal free of charge. Yours very truly, (171)

5

Dear Ms. Mitchell:

Attached is a list of the fees that you will be expected to pay at closing. In addition[1] to the real estate taxes, there is a charge for originating the loan in the lending institution. It[2] amounts to two points, which is 2 percent of the total mortgage. This fee is to be paid in cash at the time of[3] the closing.

As the buyer of the property, you are also expected to pay a fee for title insurance,[4] for the appraisal of the property, and for recording the deed and the mortgage. The only remaining[5] fee is for verification of your credit standing.

These are routine costs that accompany the purchase of[6] a mortgage. If you have other questions regarding terms of the sale, please call me any time. Since I am your[7] realtor, I will certainly be present at the closing. Sincerely, (152)

LESSON
44

1

Dear Dr. Nelson:

Congratulations upon being selected superintendent of the county school[1] system. We are delighted to be among the first residents to welcome you to our city.

Now that you have[2] accepted this position, you probably have already started thinking about the kind of house you want for your[3] family. As a newcomer to this community, you will want to choose a realtor whose advice you can[4] rely upon. Our agency is one of the oldest in this area. Last year we sold more than $10 million[5] in commercial and residential real estate.

As a partner in this agency, I have served this community[6] for almost 20 years. I am very familiar with this city and its surrounding areas. I know[7] that I can locate the perfect house for your family.

Please give me a call so that we can discuss your[8] situation. I would like to help you resolve your housing question as soon as possible. Sincerely yours,[9] (180)

2

Dear Mr. Murphy:

I am enclosing the extra set of keys to your new home. Knowing your ability to[1] get things done quickly, I would be willing to bet that you are completely settled by now.

River Road is a[2] beautiful area, and I am sure you will enjoy residing there. To help you get acquainted with your neighbors,[3] I have sent cards to their homes announcing your arrival.

In regard to your question about the property taxes,[4] you may file for an exemption after January 1. Your taxes for this year have already been paid[5] in full, and the exemption does not go into effect until six months after the title to the property[6] has been transferred to the new owner.

It has been my pleasure to represent you in making these arrangements. When[7] the need arises, I am always ready to help. Yours truly, (151)

3

Dear Miss Leonard:

The board of managers approved your loan this afternoon. The property has been appraised, and your[1] credit rating has been verified. You will receive a 20-year mortgage that is payable in monthly[2] installments. If you decide to include your homeowner insurance and property taxes with your house payments,[3] we can make those arrangements.

I know that you had some questions about acquiring an abstract for the property.[4] Because an abstract can become quite lengthy and expensive, I recommend that you purchase title insurance[5] instead. The title insurance will guarantee that your financial investment is protected.

At the time of the[6] closing, you will receive a schedule of payments. That schedule will show a breakdown of the interest and principal[7] over the 20-year period. I will be looking forward to talking with you again. Cordially yours,[8] (160)

4

Dear Mr. Morgan:

The land which adjoins your property is now being offered for sale. The current owner, who[1] has moved out of town, has asked me to supervise the sale.

The site is approximately five and a half acres;[2] I am having it surveyed to establish the exact boundaries. For all practical purposes, the boundary[3] extends east from County Road 903 to the creek and south to the woods. A stone wall marks the border on the north.[4]

At one time you were interested in purchasing this property. Would you like to discuss it further? I would[5] be happy to meet with you and walk over the land. Since this property is already zoned for residential[6] housing, it certainly could be subdivided into smaller lots.

The survey and title search will be[7] completed within three to four weeks. Please feel free to call me at any time. Yours truly, (155)

5

Dear Mr. and Mrs. Marshall:

Enclosed is a copy of my request for title insurance for the property[1] you are purchasing. The title insurance policy will be written for the amount of the sale price of the[2] property. According to the county

clerk, it should take no longer than 20 working days to have the policy[3] in hand. Therefore, there is no reason to think that the closing will be delayed by this action.

In our earlier[4] discussions several weeks ago, we talked about the possibility that more than one easement exists[5] on your lot. It now appears that the electric company has an easement that runs along the property[6] line on the west side. It is also likely that the water company has an easement along the front of the[7] property bordering the street. However, the title insurance policy will show us exactly where these[8] easements lie.

I am delighted that things are going well for you. If I can assist you in the moving[9] preparations, please call. If I don't hear from you between now and the closing, I will see you both then. Sincerely yours,[10] (200)

LESSON
45

1

MEMO TO: Howard Logan

The date of our meeting at the bank has been changed from Tuesday to Wednesday, May 3. I[1] am asking all members of the finance committee to be present at that meeting. Our first priority of[2] business will be to determine the final terms of sale. Although the zoning commission rejected our request[3] to rezone that property for apartments, we have submitted an appeal. Several developments have occurred[4] since that decision was made, and the director of public works now feels that our request will be granted.

As[5] treasurer of our corporation, you will want to open two accounts in our name. One is to be an escrow[6] account, which will be used to protect all donations and investments. The other should be a standard checking account[7] to be used for regular transactions and expenses.

If you have any problem with the new date, please let[8] me know right away. (164)

2

Dear Gerald:

Here is the progress report you requested on the building that formerly was owned by the athletic[1] club. Title to the property is still in the hands of the bank. Shortly after the facility was closed,[2] a group of local investors made an offer to purchase it. That offer was refused by the bank. Three months ago[3] a second group of investors approached the bank. This group obtained a 90-day option to purchase, which expires[4] February 9.

The terms of the option agreement clearly state that it will not be possible to get[5] an extension after the expiration date. The investors have initiated an effort to raise[6] additional funds to renovate the building. Plans are being made to open a family fitness center that[7] will include indoor swimming, jogging, tennis, and other programs.

If you would like additional information,[8] I can put you in touch with the president of this group. The membership drive will begin immediately, so[9] I would advise you to act quickly. Sincerely, (189)

3

Dear Ms. Roberts:

I am writing to inform you that a title search is now in progress for the house and three lots[1] at 48 Elm Street. The changes you requested have been added to the contract, and I am enclosing a[2] copy of the final draft.

As you know, closing is scheduled for noon, April 22, in the offices of[3] Central Savings Bank. I will meet you there.

If you have further questions regarding fees that are payable at the[4] time of closing, please call me immediately. The enclosed list is a summary of the items we discussed[5] in our last telephone conversation. As you can see, the earnest money will be withdrawn from the escrow account[6] at the time of closing. It will indeed be included in your down payment.

If you have difficulty reaching[7] me by phone, please leave a message with my secretary, Lisa. She will always know where to reach me on short[8] notice. Very truly yours, (165)

4

Dear Mrs. Barnett:

Your offer has been accepted; we can now arrange for the purchase of your new home.

I am[1] delighted that we were able to locate the house of your choice within the price range that you had specified.[2] As we said before, it offers the exact things you were looking for. I think you will find that the neighborhood is[3] quiet and conveniently located.

If you are certain that you want to pay cash for the house, we can make the[4] arrangements immediately. The current owners are eager to move, and they will gladly relinquish possession[5] whenever you wish.

I hope you will continue to think about the advantages of obtaining a mortgage[6] for this purchase. I will certainly be available to discuss this alternative with you. Cordially,[7] (140)

5

Dear Mr. and Mrs. Williams:

The couple who purchased the apartment building from you, Mr. and Mrs. Nelson,[1] informed me yesterday that they are planning to sell the property. They asked me to list the building for them,[2] and I agreed to do so.

Please be assured that the resale of this property will not cause any difficulties[3] for you. Since the owners bought the apartments on a contract basis, they will be paying off that contract in[4] full at the time of the sale. You may recall that the contract specifies that the contract cannot be assumed by[5] subsequent owners.

Before entering into a contract sale with another party, the Nelsons are aware[6] that they must terminate the contract with you. Therefore, they are preparing to require that the purchasers take out[7] a conventional mortgage.

I will keep you informed of everything that happens. Yours truly, (156)

LESSON

46

1

Dear Mr. Marvin:

We have heard that your business is experiencing a period of rapid growth and[1] prosperity. Congratulations on your success!

Your company is in a strong position today because[2] you have kept your plant modern by buying new equipment regularly. With your current volume of business, your[3] equipment will be carrying a heavier load than it has in the past.

Replacement parts and repairs are[4] expensive. Let us help you avoid mechanical problems that cause delays in production. Our experts can keep your[5] equipment in good working order. We are noted for supplying immediate service when emergencies[6] arise.

The enclosed brochure lists the types of service contracts we offer. Why not let us help you choose a plan to suit[7] your needs? We can ensure that your machinery will continue to operate efficiently. Very truly[8] yours, (161)

2

Dear Mr. Harvey:

Here is the data you requested. As you can see, it contains a complete listing of the[1] new equipment you wish to install in the firm of Jackson and Jackson, Ltd. I would like to suggest that[2] you bring your employees to our plant to see the equipment in operation. We have a very impressive[3] display of computer technology under one roof.

We would be happy to demonstrate the flexibility[4] of our units. I think we could also convince your employees that our programs are easy to use. We can[5] help them plan the types of work stations that are appropriate for their needs.

We invite you and your employees to[6] visit us at a time that is most convenient for your group. We will plan to provide a thorough orientation[7] to our equipment. Yours very truly, (148)

3

MEMO TO: All Supervisors

From time to time it is necessary to remind your employees that all safety[1] regulations must be observed. Unless you have already done so in the last three months, please call a meeting[2] with the leaders of all production teams to review these regulations in detail. Be sure to emphasize any[3] regulations which apply only to your specific areas.

Unfortunately, employees may become[4] careless in their work habits if we do not make an effort to enforce safety regulations. Remind your[5] workers to wear protective clothing, to keep work stations clean, and to keep all doorways and walkways free of obstructions.[6]

If these simple rules are followed by everyone, they will help prevent injuries and will help make our plant a[7] safe and pleasant place in which to work. (146)

4

Dear Mrs. Miller:

We are pleased that you have elected to become one of our distributors. In addition[1] to the materials which you already have, I am enclosing a copy of our newest catalog.[2] As you can see, it provides a description of each stock item that is available to you.

I am also[3] enclosing a copy of the contract for your signature. As I explained in my recent meeting with you, this[4] document does not replace the memo of agreement you have already signed. The purpose of the memo is to[5] clarify our policies and to establish the basis for a friendly business relationship. The contract[6] specifies the obligations and responsibilities that each of us shares with the other.

When you wish to[7] place an order, you may handle it directly with Kevin Harvey, our director of sales. If you wish to[8] discuss your contract in general, please feel free to contact me at any time. Cordially yours, (176)

5

MEMO TO: All Employees

It is time to renew our pledges to the city fund drive. During the past five years,[1] employees in our company have made it a point to participate in this fund drive. Because we had more[2] participants than any other industry in this city, we achieved a rare distinction last year.

You may[3] already realize how important these funds are. They are used to supplement health programs, to provide extra[4] funds for social agencies, and to maintain many worthwhile organizations that could not exist without our[5] financial help.

Only you, the employee, can make this plan work. Please demonstrate your support by contributing your[6] share. Remember that a donation from you says that you want your company to continue to be the leading[7] contributor. (143)

LESSON
47

1

Gentlemen:

Dealers from all over the city have learned how to increase their volume of sales in one easy step.[1] They have subscribed to the service we offer for arranging sales displays.

How does this service work, and what are the[2] benefits to you? If you have a contract for our services, we assume complete responsibility for[3] arranging attractive displays for store counters and windows. We will begin by creating a plan that incorporates[4] your ideas and preferences. We will ask you to list the items you wish to emphasize for each[5] display.

Then we will present our final plan for your consideration. If it meets with your approval, we will[6] assemble and disassemble the display at the appropriate times.

Our clients have found our arrangements[7] to be colorful, imaginative, and very effective. After you have had an opportunity to read[8] the enclosed brochure, give us an opportunity to show you an example of our work.

We would be delighted[9] to include you among our many satisfied customers. Very truly yours, (195)

2

MEMO TO: All Employees

The mail room supervisor tells me that our mail system is being delayed[1] unnecessarily because of mechanical problems. As a result, we are experiencing problems in[2] processing the mail before the end of the day.

As you know, the mail delivery cart is powered by an[3] electronic system. To keep it running efficiently, we must be sure that supplies, equipment, and other[4] possessions are not left in the hallways. Even a small object is capable of bringing the automatic cart[5] to a halt. When mail room personnel realize that the cart has not returned, they must locate the cart and correct the[6] problem.

We would appreciate your cooperation in aiding our mail system. (135)

3

MEMO TO: Linda Charles

It is our pleasure to welcome you as a representative of our firm. Your previous[1] experience in home furnishings provides you with excellent qualifications for this position. I am[2] certain that you will re-

cruit new dealerships for us at a record rate.

We are shipping 200 catalogs[3] to you via Federal Parcel Service. You should have them by Thursday or Friday at the latest. Please distribute[4] these catalogs among the dealers to show the variety and quality of our merchandise. We will[5] support your sales efforts by providing dependable and prompt delivery of all orders.

Please accept[6] our best wishes for a successful sales campaign. We look forward to a long and enjoyable partnership with[7] you. (141)

4

Dear Mr. Jenkins:

Thank you for your letter concerning the design of assembly parts. The answer to your question[1] is yes. Our company is capable of producing the kind of equipment needed to supplement your[2] operation. I have arranged for our regional office to send a representative to meet with you[3] personally. You will receive a call from that person within a few days to set up an appointment.

We must start[4] at the original design and follow through to product engineering in order to give you the kind of[5] precision control that you have specified. If your ultimate goal is to decrease the unit cost of your product,[6] we must design a more efficient means of production. It is unlikely that these changes would require more[7] than six months.

Again, thank you for contacting us. Our company makes thousands of parts each year, and we are eager[8] to serve you. Cordially yours, (165)

5

Dear Mr. Hudson:

There is a control system that can save

money in fuel efficiency and earn money[1] for you by increasing production. We are talking about the national leader in sales and service, Bestway[2] Control System.

Whether your products are made from gas, liquid, or powder material, this system provides[3] technology that will improve the overall operation of your plant. We can reduce your costs, improve product[4] uniformity, and increase your profits.

May we demonstrate how our improved system can be applied to your[5] manufacturing plant? We have a staff of experts who will conduct a study at no charge to you. We have[6] provided these services to many types of industries whose products vary from plastics to nuclear power[7] generators.

I will call your office to make an appointment, Mr. Hudson. Yours truly, (156)

LESSON
48

1

Dear Ms. Temple:

By now you should have received the new shipment of merchandise. I am writing to express our[1] appreciation for your patience and understanding. When I heard that the original shipment contained[2] several damaged items, I was very disturbed. I knew that you needed these items to replenish your shelf stock[3] and that I had guaranteed an early delivery to you.

We would like to make a special offer to help[4] compensate for any inconvenience that you may have experienced. For your next purchase of our products, we will[5]

include a complimentary case of our top-selling product, the hand and body lotion. You may have this[6] product in either of two sizes. I know that you normally stock the 32-ounce bottle and the 4-ounce jar.[7] We will comply with whichever request you make.

Thank you again for your continued patronage. Sincerely yours,[8] (160)

2

Dear Mr. Jason:

This letter is to remind you that your payments for Invoices 342 and 701 are[1] now overdue. The total amount owed to us is $5,682.49.[2]

In the original agreement signed by the manager of your store, you were to make partial payments[3] on the first day of March, April, and May to bring your account up to date. We received one payment on March 7 for[4] $1,500. Since that date, however, you have not responded to our letters or calls.[5]

The remainder of your account must be paid in full. If we do not receive this payment within ten working days[6] following your receipt of this certified letter, we will be forced to place this matter in the hands of a[7] collection agency.

We would be very sorry to initiate such action. Please mail us your check now. Very[8] truly yours, (162)

3

Dear Mr. Chester:

Thank you for your letter regarding our recent sales campaign. It was gratifying to learn[1] that you have experienced a great deal of success with our line of building products. It is not uncommon to[2] hear that our distributors are pleased with the sales of our products. Because these promotions have proved to be very[3] effective, we will be sponsoring similar events in the future.

Since you have had so much success with our[4] building materials, would you like to expand your inventory by carrying our lawn and garden[5] materials? The grass seed, which is available only in 50-pound bags, outsold many competitive products[6] last year.

I am including a packet of materials describing the lawn and garden products. We have[7] found our garden products to be very complementary with our building materials. Yours very truly,[8] (160)

4

Dear Mr. Turner:

We have reviewed a report from the representatives who attended the factory[1] demonstration you conducted at the national convention.

As a result of seeing the data you[2] presented, we have decided to add the line of products you introduced at the convention. We feel that our sales[3] force can bring in orders that will justify the addition of this equipment to our line.

We do have several[4] questions relating to the conditions you have listed for warranty protection. Would you be available[5] to discuss these details with our sales and marketing staff? If you cannot visit our offices personally,[6] perhaps I could arrange for a teleconference call. Such a call would allow all parties to communicate[7] freely.

Please let me know how I should proceed. Very truly yours, (151)

5

Dear Miss Sterling:

Thank you for your letter explaining your financial circumstances.

Although we do not usually[1] grant extensions on accounts, we feel that this is a special case. Therefore, we are granting an additional[2] 90 days of credit on your loan. Since we do not plan to increase the rate of interest for this additional[3] debt service, it will not be necessary to draw up a new contract. However, a formal agreement[4] is being prepared to set forth the terms of the extension. You will have to sign this agreement before it[5] can go into effect.

I understand that the growth of your company will depend directly upon acquiring[6] the new facility that you are in the process of buying. The only request we have is that you provide[7] us with a copy of that purchase agreement.

The extension papers will be ready tomorrow afternoon,[8] June 1. You may come in any time to sign them. Yours very truly, (173)

LESSON
49

1

Dear Customer:

The enclosed booklet will introduce you to our new line of folding chairs. Please note that these are not[1] ordinary chairs. They differ from many competitive brands in that they are constructed from the finest[2] materials. They are designed for both indoor and outdoor use.

Your customers will like them for many reasons.[3] These chairs are appropriate for business use, but they will look almost as good in a residential setting. They[4] don't require extra protection; they are as sturdy as they are attractive.

We are accepting trial orders for[5] a minimum of 12 chairs with payment due within 90 days. We are confident that you will share our excitement[6] once you have seen our product. Return the chairs within 30 days if they do not prove to be moneymakers.[7] To illustrate my confidence in this product, I predict that you will be ready to reorder within[8] 30 days.

You may place your order any time between 8 a.m. and 4:30 p.m. We will look forward to[9] your call. Sincerely yours, (184)

2

MEMO TO: All Employees

Thanks to the efforts of our research committee, we can now announce new options in[1] your insurance benefits. These options represent important modifications in your total health care plan.[2]

Beginning on July 1, dental coverage will be added for a small monthly fee. The amount of the fee[3] will depend upon the number of members in your family.

In addition, your policy will cover[4] specific types of oral surgery that have not previously been included. Please read the attached booklet[5] carefully to determine what expenses will be covered. If you have specific questions, please bring them directly[6] to the personnel office.

Again, we wish to thank the research committee for helping us achieve these improvements[7] in our insurance program. (146)

3

Dear Mr. Harrison:

Thank you for your check for $895.17 in payment of[1] our Invoice 8093. Your remittance arrived 15 days after the end of the discount period.[2] Therefore, your payment should have been $913.44. You may

forward a check for the[3] additional $18.27 or include that amount with your next monthly payment. If you[4] choose the latter method of payment, please provide a notation that the additional amount is to be[5] credited to your unpaid balance for April.

In the meantime, we are crediting your account for a total of[6] $895.17. Your next installment should be received by May 6 in order to[7] qualify you for the discount for that month.

If you require further assistance, please call us at the number listed[8] above in our letterhead. Very truly yours, (168)

4

MEMO TO: All Employees

Six weeks ago we announced a new incentive plan based on the concept of profit[1] sharing. We are delighted to report that the success of this plan has surpassed all expectations. Because of[2] the combined efforts of everyone, production has increased by 18 percent. Congratulations on a job[3] well done.

In addition to increased production, an emphasis on improved procedures has reduced the rate of[4] errors by a substantial margin. If we continue at this rate, our year-end financial report will hold a[5] special surprise for every employee.

This kind of plan helps each of us to realize our contributions to[6] the company. Individually and collectively, we are having a direct effect on the success[7] of this corporation. (144)

5

Dear Mrs. Hastings:

Our new line of merchandise will soon be ready for marketing, but is the market ready[1] for us?

As you know, it has been characteristic of our company to emphasize expert workmanship and[2] traditional styling for all of our products. When we have designed past advertising campaigns, we have directed[3] our message to a traditional audience.

Now we would like to depart from that image. We would like to[4] have you prepare an ad campaign that would appeal especially to the young professional market.

We have always[5] been very satisfied with your ideas, Mrs. Hastings, and we are confident that you will be able[6] to provide us with the right direction once again. I am always available to discuss ideas with[7] you. Please call me at your convenience. Yours truly, (149)

LESSON

50

1

MEMO TO: All Managers

An order has been placed for new assembly machines, and we expect delivery[1] within three weeks. Since these machines will increase production by 13 to 15 percent, all managers will need[2] to make adjustments in scheduling. Such changes will be necessary to keep parts flowing to the assembly[3] machines.

I suggest that you meet with your employees in small groups to explain why procedures must be changed. Please[4] assure everyone that these automated machines will not cause the loss of any jobs. As a matter of fact,[5] we will need to hire additional people in several areas.

We are arranging special training sessions[6] which will be conducted shortly after the equipment is installed. These sessions will be administered by[7] representatives of the manufacturer. In general, the operation and maintenance of this new[8] machinery will not differ greatly from that of the past.

If you wish to have assistance in explaining these[9] matters to your employees, a member of our engineering staff will be happy to help. (196)

2

Dear Ms. Doyle:

Thank you for your order of August 7. The 30 coats you requested will be shipped to you without[1] delay. Although we cannot give you an exact date for delivery, we will do all we can to have the[2] merchandise to you in time for your fall sale.

It will take us approximately ten days to process your order[3] and prepare the items for shipping. Once a shipment leaves our loading area, it takes about five days in transit.[4] If all things go according to schedule, you should have the coats within two weeks.

We will send the order c.o.d.[5] Although I do not know exactly how much the freight charges will be, I can tell you that the trucking company[6] we use charges a minimum of $50 for all merchandise under 100 pounds.

If there are[7] any unusual delays, I will be certain to let you know. Very truly yours, (156)

3

Dear Mr. Hamilton:

Thank you for contacting Empire Roofing, Inc. We appreciate your[1] interest in becoming a distributor for our firm.

Our standard procedure is to send a representative[2] to visit your retail outlet. During this visit our representative will explain our policies and[3] collect the information we need to make a routine analysis. You will have the opportunity to[4] ask questions at that time.

We will contact you personally approximately three weeks following the visit.[5] If your place of business has the qualifications necessary to become a distributorship, we will[6] ask you to sign a contract agreement that will become effective immediately.

You will be contacted[7] by phone to set up an appointment for the visit. Cordially yours, (152)

4

Gentlemen:

This letter is to inform you of recent price changes for all leather products. Because of rising[1] costs of raw materials, we have incurred higher manufacturing costs. As a result, we must now increase[2] our factory prices by 15 percent.

We are enclosing a cost sheet that lists the price changes for each item[3] of stock. Please be certain to use the figures on this sheet in placing all future orders.

We are continuing[4] to see a high demand for leather goods. Because of a projected shortage in raw materials, that demand[5] will be even greater.

We encourage you to place your orders as early as possible. We will do our[6] best to fill them to your satisfaction. Yours truly, (129)

5

Dear Ms. Richards:

We still have not received payments from you for January, February, and March. Our records[1] show that the invoices were mailed to you, but we have received no response in spite of repeated requests. Is there[2] a good explanation for this delay in payment?

We have enjoyed a good relationship with your business for[3] more than eight years. There have been times when your bookkeeping department has fallen behind in its work, but it is[4] unusual to have the problem reach this extreme point.

We would like to continue our relationship with your[5] company. However, an understanding must be reached concerning this problem. Before we can process orders[6] in the future, we must agree upon a more satisfactory system of making payments. Very truly yours,[7] (140)

LESSON

51

1

Dear Mr. Vincent:

In a retail establishment as busy as yours, the sales personnel must work quickly. They[1] need to determine the correct retail price of all products within seconds. They also need to quote schedules[2] for deliveries and to confirm orders upon short notice.

Can your sales staff provide this information[3] immediately?

If the answer is no, then you need to have a system which will do this work for your employees.[4] As a manufacturer of the leading products in information processing, we can design a system[5] for you which will improve your business administration in many ways. It will provide greater control over your[6] basic operation.

It will increase the efficiency and accuracy of records management.

If you[7] are thinking that such systems are out of reach for small businesses like yours, the best news is yet to come. Our systems[8] usually pay for themselves within five years.

Make an appointment now to look at the equipment that we have[9] available. Sincerely yours, (186)

2

MEMO TO: Richard Lincoln

Yesterday I received a memo from you stating that you have not been given credit[1] for the sales contracts you delivered in January. I have requested a printout of your sales reports to check them against our master records. I should have an answer for you by tomorrow.

We have been modifying[3] our information system, and it is possible that some of your sales were not transmitted into the central[4] memory bank. Implementing new systems can cause problems, but such problems are temporary. Also, the[5] end result is generally worth the confusion created by changing our procedures.

It is clearly an[6] advantage to be able to process your orders in half the time previously required. If you have any[7] further problems, call me right away. (146)

3

Dear Executive:

Have you been looking at the new software programs currently on the market and wondering[1] which would offer the best advantages for your personal and professional use?

Our factory representatives[2] make personal visits to business locations for business managers like you. They bring the equipment[3] necessary to provide demonstrations of our computers and software products.

May we put one of our[4] representatives in touch with you? In this busy age of competing products and services, it is important[5] to have a thorough orientation that is given by an expert in the field. That is why we employ only[6] knowledgeable people to make these demonstrations for us.

An agent will be contacting you soon. A visit[7] from this person will offer opportunities that you didn't know existed. Yours very truly, (159)

4

MEMO TO: Elizabeth Preston

Thank you for the excellent suggestions you made at lunch yesterday. I agree[1] that some changes are needed in the flow of information throughout our offices. Would you be willing to[2] serve on a committee to look into modifications of our system?

I would like the committee to conduct[3] a complete study of the needs of each office. I would hope that your report would include an analysis[4] of efficiency, accuracy, and control. I would also like to have recommendations for solutions[5] to the problems that are identified in the report.

If it is the recommendation of the committee[6] that we need to upgrade our equipment, that suggestion will be given serious consideration. However,[7] I would expect to see documentation for this request. (151)

5

Dear Mrs. Williams:

As a good customer of our store, you know that we always carry the finest office[1] equipment. We are proud to announce that we have added a new line of office furniture that was especially[2] designed for modular equipment.

These attractive units are reasonably priced, and they can be arranged to[3] suit your individual requirements. If you wish to add a terminal to the system you are now using,[4] we have component parts that will accommodate your needs. If you plan to purchase a completely new system for[5] information processing, we can design a layout for you.

We would like to have you visit our showroom this week.[6] If you will notify my office first, I will be certain to be here when you come. Sincerely yours, (138)

LESSON
52

1

Dear Sir or Madam:

An excellent word processor can produce attractive printed copy. Even the most[1] capable machine, however, is limited by the abilities of the person dictating the letter.[2]

If the person who originates the correspondence uses a poor choice of words, the letter will sound awkward.[3] If the writing is too wordy or unclear, much of the message will be lost unnecessarily.

On the other[4] hand, why not emphasize to your employees the importance of improving their communication skills? If you[5] subscribe to our communications newsletter, we will provide the guidance for writing effectively.

If you[6] return the attached form within ten days, you will be eligible for our intro-

ductory rate. Subscribe now[7] and save 20 percent. Very truly yours, (148)

2

Dear Sir:

I am writing to acknowledge that the shipment we received from you this morning arrived on schedule.[1] However, it was incomplete. We had asked for the following items:

1. Four cartons of cloth ribbons for the[2] Model 700 printer.
2. One No. 900 daisy wheel.
3. Nine boxes of disks.

Although the invoice[3] listed the items shown above, we discovered later that two boxes of disks had been omitted. Therefore,[4] I am requesting that you forward the remaining disks to our office.

I would appreciate it if you could[5] ship the missing items without delay. Although we are not in the habit of placing rush orders, we had[6] anticipated having these in stock by now. Please let us know when to expect delivery. Sincerely yours,[7] (140)

3

MEMO TO: Susan Carter

Will you please check to make sure that the computer program we use for inventory[1] control is working properly?

Yesterday I learned that we are nearly out of the 20-pound paper. Last week[2] we discovered that other supplies were dangerously low. If our data base were current, these unexpected[3] shortages would not have occurred.

As you know, we cannot afford to run short of office supplies. Such a shortage[4] results in delays and could cause us to miss delivery deadlines. Anything that prevents us from offering[5] dependable service is a serious problem for us.

I know that I can rely on you. When you isolate[6] the problem, please let me know right away. (128)

4

Dear Mr. Roberts:

Since installing the new computer hardware two years ago, our needs have grown tremendously.[1] In fact, our needs have far surpassed the capabilities of the hardware.

Before adding new terminals and printers[2] to our current equipment, we would like to have an up-to-date analysis of our needs. In addition[3] to the data already being processed, we would like to add inventory control and various sales programs.[4] Also, our regional sales people should be able to have direct access to the central computer.

Would[5] you be willing to **provide** this analysis for us? We invite you to come to our office and discuss these[6] problems with us. I would appreciate it if you could let me know **within** the next few days. Sincerely yours,[7] (140)

provide: conduct, do, perform
within: during, in

5

MEMO TO: Jennifer Ford

Enclosed is a printout of your sales record for the past year. I thought you would enjoy[1] seeing the total figures in print. As our most successful sales representative this year, Jennifer, you are[2] to be congratulated for your performance.

As you know, there is much more to selling computer equipment[3] than making the initial sale. The distributors expect our sales people to have a great deal of

technical[4] knowledge about the product. After the sale has been finalized, they depend upon our representatives for[5] advice and follow-up services. Therefore, it should come as no surprise that we employ only highly qualified[6] personnel to perform these important functions.

We appreciate the amount of effort and quality[7] of performance that you have brought to our organization. Thank you for your example of excellence. (159)

LESSON
53

1

Dear Mrs. Sheldon:

Thank you for your inquiry concerning new software for your office information system.[1] We can provide you with various programs to meet the needs described in your letter. I am enclosing a[2] catalog which describes the options that are available.

Our contract with you specifies that you will receive a[3] discount on every order placed after your orders have reached a minimum of $2,000 per year. Because[4] you exceeded that amount with the placement of your last order, this discount goes into effect immediately.[5] Therefore, all future invoices for this year will reflect a discount of 20 percent.

We appreciate[6] your continued support for our products. Please let me know if you need further information in selecting[7] software programs. Sincerely yours, (146)

2

Gentlemen:

When you purchased the computer equipment in your office, you probably signed a service contract.[1] When you entered into that agreement, you hoped that your service problems would be solved. Have you found that you now receive[2] the quick and reliable service needed to keep your equipment operating efficiently? Have you[3] found that the service agreement you signed with the manufacturer of your equipment is as economical[4] and satisfactory as it should be?

If you cannot answer yes to both of these questions, we have a solution[5] that will greatly increase productivity in your office. It is our business to keep information systems[6] operating at their top level of efficiency. We service hardware and make repairs when necessary.[7] We carry a full line of parts and accessories from nine major manufacturers.

Although most equipment[8] is built to endure a great deal of wear, even the sturdiest unit requires regular maintenance[9] to keep it in good condition.

To learn more about our services, please return the postage-paid card that we have[10] enclosed. Yours truly, (204)

3

MEMO TO: Ralph Wilson

Having just read your report, I agree with your recommendations for sharing computer[1] time with other companies. If we subscribe to a time-share system, we could have the use of a very expensive[2] main frame for a cost that is relatively inexpensive.

As a member of this network, how would we be[3] charged for our usage? I know that we would share the expense with other companies like ours, but are we charged a[4] flat rate? How are the charges determined, and how frequent are the payments?

As I consider the many discussions[5] we have had on reducing operating costs, I am inclined to try the time-share system. Please investigate[6] whether or not we can subscribe for a trial period before entering into a full contract agreement.[7] (141)

4

MEMO TO: Nancy Harper

When we met yesterday, I explained that we will need to have color graphs for the budget[1] report that is **due** next week. However, I may not have explained that we will need additional information[2] for the report. We will need the following items: a profit and loss statement for the new line of software,[3] a printout that compares this year's earnings with those of previous years, and projected earnings for the next five years.[4]

The report should be printed and bound. I know that this represents a substantial amount of work and preparation,[5] but it is necessary that we present this information. To help you with this project, I am assigning[6] two employees from our word processing department to work with you. You will also have full use of a conference[7] room until your work is **completed.**

If you have questions, please bring them to me at any time. (158)

due: needed, expected
completed: finished, done

5

MEMO TO: Margaret Roy

We have had many problems with the accounting software we purchased in February.[1] After giving much consideration to this issue, I have decided that this software cannot do the[2] work we require. It is not comprehensive enough to meet our needs. Furthermore, it would be an expensive mistake[3] to continue using it.

There are several other systems that might work, but we are hesitant to make[4] a decision until we have had a chance to compare the performance of each. It might be possible to rent[5] sample programs for a limited period of time. Because it is important to choose the right system,[6] I feel that it would be worthwhile to experiment. I know that trying different systems means that our employees[7] will have to adjust to many changes in procedures. However, we do not want to make the same mistake of[8] purchasing the wrong product.

Please give me your reactions to this plan. (172)

LESSON
54

1

Dear Mr. Chambers:

We have experienced serious problems with the last order of disks that we received from[1] you. We have used 47 of the 100 disks that we ordered. Unfortunately, three of those used have[2] proved to be damaged. They appeared to be functioning in the beginning, but we have actually lost entire[3] files on those disks.

We are returning the damaged disks along with the 53 unused disks. We hope that you can[4] recover the information contained on the damaged disks. We would like to have you replace the disks we are[5] returning with entirely new merchandise. Will you test the new disks to establish their reliability?[6]

The problems caused by these damaged disks have resulted in a substantial expense and inconvenience for our[7] com-

pany. We would like to be compensated for this expense. What do you suggest? Very truly yours, (157)

2

MEMO TO: Brenda Mitchell

Thank you for your excellent remarks at the staff meeting this morning. You were quite right[1] to bring up the suggestion that we review our plans for remodeling the central records office. Although we[2] drew up these plans nearly a year ago, we seem to have forgotten to follow up on this matter.

I would like[3] to have you study those plans carefully. If you believe that they are appropriate and adequate for our current[4] and future needs, I will have the business office send them out for bids immediately. Since drawing up those[5] plans, we have changed our procedures for storing records. We have come to rely more upon disks for storage, and we[6] now rely less upon hard copy. Do the renovation plans allow enough space for storage of electronic[7] media, and is that space adequately defined?

When we make these structural changes, we should be certain[8] that the changes will accommodate our needs for several years to come. (173)

3

Dear Mr. Baxter:

During the last six months, we have had a problem in transmitting electronic mail. The problem[1] seems to occur only between our central headquarters and our branch offices located overseas. On[2] one occasion last week, an entire series of important documents was lost during a transmittal that[3] originated in Germany.

Fortunately, we were able to recover

most of the copy in time[4] for the meeting that was scheduled for that afternoon. However, this problem must be corrected before it results[5] in serious consequences.

I believe that the problem must be mechanical. We have gone over our[6] operating guide very carefully, and we cannot locate any error in our procedures. Since our[7] equipment is still covered by warranty, could you send someone immediately to identify and correct[8] the problem? Sincerely yours, (164)

4

MEMO TO: Word Processing Operators

Welcome to this training session. You are here to receive an introduction[1] to the new software for our word processing department. The attached training manual will show you how[2] to use your terminal for creating, editing, printing, and storing documents.

After completing this[3] manual, you will be able to use your work station to produce documents that look very professional. Yet,[4] these documents will require less than half the time you have previously **needed** to produce finished copy. You[5] will be able to work quickly, independently, and confidently.

This equipment is designed to make your[6] work as easy and free of **errors** as possible. Please feel free to ask questions as we work through the exercises[7] contained in this manual. (146)

needed: taken, required
errors: mistakes, problems

5

Dear Ms. Evans:

Enclosed are three new disks containing copy which we transferred from the damaged disks. When you review[1] the document index for each disk, you will see that we were able to recover most of the missing copy[2] that was lost when your old disks were damaged.

Our analysts believe that the damage resulted from improper care[3] of the disks. As we explained during the training sessions, disks require careful handling and special arrangements[4] for storage. If you store them properly, you will greatly reduce the risk of damage.

Occasionally, however,[5] a disk is damaged for no apparent reason. That is why it is advisable to make more than one copy[6] of every disk you use. The extra copy can prevent much worry and aggravation.

We are glad that we[7] could help. Please call on us at any time. Cordially yours, (150)

LESSON ▬▬▬▬▬

55

1

Dear Executive:

We are pleased to invite you to a seminar for retail businesses. The purpose of this[1] seminar will be to show owners and managers how they can use their computer equipment to achieve greater[2] efficiency in their overall operation.

The enclosed brochure describes the various functions that[3] will be discussed. As you can see, there are many ways in which your equipment can be used to exercise more[4] control over every aspect of your operation.

Although you can attend this workshop

for a very[5] reasonable fee, enrollments are limited. Send your registration today. In order to reserve a place for[6] you and other members of your management team, a deposit must be included for each person.

We will be[7] looking forward to having you join us. Sincerely yours, (150)

2

MEMO TO: Bill Carver

Due to increases in the cost of paper and printing services, we may need to make[1] changes in our operating budget.

This decision will be made at the budget meeting on Friday. Please run[2] an analysis of payroll, inventory, advertising, and other overhead costs. Prepare six copies[3] of your report and distribute them to all department heads by noon on Thursday.

After we have all had an[4] opportunity to study the report and to prepare some recommendations, we will establish a plan for[5] reducing costs. Please give this project priority over all other activities. I know that this is a[6] particularly busy time right now, but it is imperative that we have this information soon. (139)

3

Dear Manager:

If your computer is not capable of producing graphic displays and printouts in color,[1] you are not getting your money's worth.

You can now purchase equipment that provides these functions. If expense is a[2] concern, you will probably find that the new software costs little more or even less than what you paid for much of[3] your original software.

Look at the enclosed examples to see what color can do for your company's[4]

communications. You can use color to highlight the individual parts of a report. You can also[5] use it to trace the expansion of departments and programs. You can use color to provide emphasis wherever[6] you wish.

Don't settle for black-and-white graphics when it is so easy and economical to have the benefits[7] of color. Call our main office at 101 Northwest Boulevard for a free demonstration. Cordially,[8] (160)

4

Dear Ms. Davenport:

Thank you for your interest in Western Electronics, Inc. Although we have[1] no openings for someone with your qualifications at this time, we will keep your letter on file.

Openings[2] occur frequently in our word processing department, and we are always interested in interviewing[3] qualified candidates. According to the resumé you **sent** to our office, you have taken several courses[4] in word processing as well as data processing. This training will serve as a valuable asset in[5] your employment search.

If you would like to make an appointment to come into our personnel office, we will arrange[6] to give you a series of tests to determine the level of your skills. You may also talk with our personnel[7] director at that time. When a position becomes available, you will be **notified.** Sincerely yours,[8] (160)

sent: mailed
notified: contacted, informed

5

MEMO TO: Robert Jackson

I am enclosing a list of new accounts to

be entered into the central[1] memory bank. Will you be certain that this information is programmed correctly?

As you may recall from recent[2] experiences, there have been some problems with the classification of information. Some operators[3] have been accessing information that is not current. The problem occurs because we have duplicate files that[4] are supposed to contain the same information. When a change is made in the master file, that change is not always[5] carried over to the other files.

We can solve this problem if we make a point of erasing all outdated,[6] duplicate files and replacing them with the new file at the time we make the change. This is an important matter,[7] and I appreciate your willingness to help. (149)

LESSON
56

1

MEMO TO: Audit Supervisors

To help refresh your knowledge of auditing procedures, we plan to offer[1] classes beginning on Monday, November 4. Please see the attached schedule of classes.

We have had a very[2] positive response to these classes in the past, and we are hoping that participation will be even greater[3] this year. As a result of the recent reorganization in this department, the workload of each auditor[4] has increased substantially. It is more important than ever for each person to use the most accurate[5] and efficient means possible to complete his or her work.

It is our agency's policy to pay the fees.[6]

Employees who attend these classes will receive one hour of college credit from the city university.[7] The final date for registration is October 22.

If you have additional questions, you may[8] call me at extension 191. (166)

2

Dear Jim:

My request for additional funding was approved by the legislature. As a result, I shall be[1] able to establish a new office in the Department of Health and Safety. When we discussed the idea[2] of this office, you expressed interest in applying for the position of director.

The new office will be[3] responsible for the coordination and management of all emergency medical services[4] in the state. This includes ambulance services offered by hospitals, fire departments, and private agencies.[5] The primary objective of the new director will be to establish and maintain a high standard of[6] quality for all emergency services.

We ordinarily post a formal announcement of this job[7] opening. All applicants will receive guidelines explaining the selection process. The final candidates will be[8] interviewed individually, and a decision will be made no later than June 1. Sincerely, (179)

3

MEMO TO: Members of the City Council

Here is the agenda for the September meeting. Please notice that[1] several city departments are requesting budget increases. I am prepared to make a strong recommendation[2] that we table these requests until we can be certain of the information presented.

A representative[3] from the hospital

foundation will address the council on the subject of medical services. It is[4] the foundation's recommendation that the city adopt a paramedic program to supplement the[5] emergency services now being offered. The board will present a formal proposal outlining the[6] administrative procedures and costs of such a program. Please take a moment to read the attached copy of[7] that proposal.

The remaining items on the agenda are self-explanatory. (156)

4

Dear Mr. Davidson:

This letter is in regard to the safety inspection which was recently **conducted**[1] in your plant. The results of that inspection are shown in the enclosed report.

In general, your plant meets the standards[2] set forth in the state guidelines. However, there are a few instances in which your company is in violation[3] of state regulations. Those violations are **shown** on page 1 of the report.

The state allows a 60-day[4] period in which these violations must be remedied. At the end of that period, the inspector[5] will return to your location to conduct a second inspection.

If you have questions regarding this report,[6] please allow me to answer them. Very truly yours, (130)

conducted: made, completed
shown: listed, given

5

Dear Property Owner:

There will be a public meeting at the county courthouse on May 4. The meeting will be[1] held in the main meeting room, and it will begin at 7:30 p.m. The purpose of the meeting will be[2] to discuss property tax assessments that are being considered by the county council.

If the proposed[3] legislation is adopted, each landowner will be charged an additional fee for each piece of property[4] owned. The amount of the fee will depend upon the amount of land that is owned. Those people owning property[5] which contains less than two acres will pay a set fee. However, those who own property having two or more acres[6] will pay a fee per acre.

If the legislation is passed, the revenue gained from these fees will be used to solve[7] the drainage problems that have occurred in various parts of the county. Any remaining funds would be used[8] to make ordinary repairs to county roads.

This is the only public meeting scheduled for this discussion. Yours[9] truly, (181)

LESSON

57

1

MEMO TO: Henry Chase

Due to the excessive amount of snow that fell last winter, the funds that had been reserved[1] for snow removal were depleted early in the year. If we have even half as much snow this winter as we[2] had last year, we will be unable to keep our streets clear.

Since every department is taking extra precautions[3] to avoid increasing its budget, I suggest that you postpone some street repairs until next summer. Of course, there[4] are some areas that require immediate attention and cannot wait that long. In other areas,[5] however, the need may be much less critical.

If we can delay these repairs until the snow season has passed,[6] we can then use the remaining funds as needed. Please give this proposal serious consideration and let me[7] know your feelings. (143)

2

Dear Mr. Richards:

I was pleased and surprised to read about our conservation efforts in your recent newspaper[1] article. Thank you for giving the readers an excellent account of the environmental problems that[2] we are facing.

I am glad that you made a point of discussing several solutions to the problems. Although[3] our department does not presume to have the correct answer every time, we do attempt to find solutions that[4] will benefit society as a whole. In order to make that choice, we weigh many factors before proposing[5] a solution.

The most important part of your message is a point worth making again and again. Conservation[6] is the responsibility of everyone. As long as you continue to educate citizens about[7] environmental issues, you are providing a public service that is beneficial to all of[8] us. Sincerely yours, (164)

3

Dear Dr. and Mrs. Conrad:

This year is the tenth anniversary of the completion of city hall. When[1] this beautiful building was added to Madison Street, it brought an entirely new look to the downtown area.[2]

As you may recall from previous publicity, the existing building represents the first phase of the[3] original building plans.

The second phase calls for an extension that would provide space for additional[4] meeting rooms. However, budgetary limitations have prevented the construction of this phase.

As a special[5] gift to celebrate the anniversary of this impressive facility, a group of citizens is[6] organizing a fund to be used toward building costs.

We know that we can count on you, a concerned citizen, to[7] contribute toward this cause. Cordially yours, (148)

4

Dear Homeowner:

The city of Jacksonville is pleased to comply with the wishes of your neighborhood association.[1] The city council has met and approved a request to widen Maple Boulevard. Two lanes—one eastbound lane[2] and one westbound lane—will be added. Construction will begin on July 11.

Although there will be a[3] temporary inconvenience during the rebuilding period, we are **convinced** that the benefits will far[4] outweigh the problems. Please watch the newspaper for news that will affect your transportation routes. We will provide advance[5] notices when streets are to be closed and when alternate routes have been **selected.**

We estimate that all construction[6] will be completed within 8 to 12 weeks. We appreciate your patience and cooperation. Yours[7] truly, (141)

convinced: certain, sure
selected: designated, chosen

5

Dear Citizen:

Urban renewal is a matter of concern to

everyone. Various areas in our[1] city have recently been designated as historical sites. People who purchase houses within these[2] areas may apply for special government loans that can be applied toward restoration of the buildings.[3] Depending upon the exact location, these houses may be zoned for commercial use or for private homes.

As part[4] of the restoration plan, the city parks department has already begun a beautification program.[5] During the next five years, the city will plant trees and flowers along the main boulevards. These plants will be maintained[6] by employees of the parks department. Priority will be given to repairing streets, sidewalks, and other[7] necessary areas.

Please join with us in an effort to beautify our city. If you would like more[8] information on how you can help, write or call our office. Sincerely yours, (173)

LESSON

58

1

Dear Walter:

It is a pleasure to congratulate you on your outstanding service to this agency. During[1] the past 30 years, you have set an example of excellence in your performance. You have served in three different[2] departments, and each of those departments has prospered under your leadership.

We all want to extend our best[3] wishes for an enjoyable and satisfying retirement. Knowing you as I do, I do not expect your[4] retirement to be a quiet one. I have no doubt that you will continue to be an active, guiding force in[5] this community. As

a matter of fact, I was delighted to learn that you have decided to serve on an[6] advisory committee for this agency.

I am certain that you will want to celebrate your retirement[7] by enjoying your new freedom for a while. After a few weeks have passed, please contact me so that I can arrange[8] for you to meet with the committee. Sincerely yours, (169)

2

MEMO TO: All Department Heads

State auditors will be with us next Monday. Please arrange your schedules so that[1] you will be free to assist them in every way.

Since they will be working on an extremely tight schedule, we are[2] requesting that you gather all necessary records in advance so that the auditors will not have to waste time[3] searching for files. We should be prepared to extend them every courtesy while they are working here.

We would prefer[4] that each department head work directly with the auditors, but it may be necessary for some of you to[5] appoint other staff members to do so. If you are planning for someone other than yourself to be present that[6] day, please be certain that he or she is well informed and can answer any questions that might arise.

After meeting[7] with me, the auditors will be introduced to members of the accounting department. They will then begin[8] their review of the data. (165)

3

Dear Mr. and Mrs. Gray:

Thank you for your recent letter of support. It is comforting to know that you and[1] many other individuals approve of the stand I have taken in regard to oil drilling. Many people[2] have written to show their support for the pending legislation. Having studied the situation carefully,[3] I am more convinced than ever that this legislation is necessary to protect the rights of our citizens.[4]

I am enclosing a brief questionnaire asking for your opinions about various bills that are facing[5] members of Congress. I would be grateful if you would take the time now to express your views about each of these[6] items. As your representative in national government, I am always appreciative when people[7] are willing to communicate their concerns to me. Cordially yours, (152)

4

MEMO TO: All Directors

I am pleased to announce that a new department has been created—the Office of[1] Development and Planning. I have appointed Judy Marshall, an experienced and capable administrator,[2] as director. She will **assume** her new duties on February 1.

The main responsibility[3] of the new department will be to coordinate all building and zoning requests. The creation of this[4] **department** will help to ensure that our city is prepared to meet the changes that are associated[5] with steady growth.

Judy is not a newcomer to our city administration. She has served as budget[6] coordinator and also as assistant director of parks. Her past experience as a volunteer in[7] this city (and in other cities in which she has resided) is further proof of her commitment to community[8] improvements.

Please join me in helping Judy feel welcome in her new capacity. (175)

assume: begin, start
department: office

5

Dear Mr. Davidson:

The city council has passed a resolution to provide a plan for renovating[1] our downtown area. We are asking only the most experienced and dedicated individuals[2] to serve on this task force. Because you are an architect whose work is widely recognized for its excellence, you would[3] bring valuable guidance to this committee. Would you agree to participate?

The objective of this[4] committee will be to conduct research, prepare a master plan, and report its recommendations to the city[5] administration in approximately one year. We are asking the committee to meet and establish[6] its primary goals early next month.

The work of this task force will be funded by a grant from local corporations,[7] and the budget information will be made available in advance of your first meeting. The mission of[8] this committee is vital to the future of our city, Mr. Davidson. If we have the benefit of your[9] knowledge and judgment, we feel certain that we will have the expertise needed to achieve our goals. Sincerely[10] yours, (201)

LESSON

59

1

Dear Mrs. Hamilton:

Thank you for writing to express interest in working for our city administration.[1] We are pleased to learn that you will be making your home here. While we are always eager to greet new citizens[2] in this community, it is especially nice to welcome people who have a background in urban affairs.[3]

I am particularly interested in your most recent project, your doctoral dissertation. The subject[4] of urban redevelopment is timely, and we are always in need of new data. If you would be so[5] kind as to mail a copy to me, I will see that it reaches the appropriate department.

We would be happy[6] to meet with you to discuss future employment. Although we do not have an opening now that requires your[7] qualifications, we are expecting to expand our Department of Urban Affairs. Perhaps there will be a[8] position for you within six months.

Please feel free to visit us the next time you are in town. Sincerely yours,[9] (180)

2

Dear Miss Edwards:

Thank you for applying for a secretarial position in the Department of Natural[1] Resources. Although we have no positions available at the present time, there may be other opportunities[2] for employment in the state office building. We suggest that you file an application with the personnel[3] division.

To submit an application, you may come to the personnel office between the hours of[4] 8 a.m. and 5 p.m. daily. After you have completed the application form, you will be asked to take[5] the standard tests to evaluate the level of your basic office skills. Following the completion of these[6] tests, you will be invited to meet and talk with a personnel counselor. That person will be able to advise[7] you about the opportunities that are available.

I hope I have answered your questions sufficiently.[8] I wish you well in your employment search. Sincerely yours, (171)

3

Dear Members of the Board:

I am writing to protest the decision to add two new traffic lanes to Elm Boulevard.[1] If you have driven through this neighborhood recently, you would know that this area is populated by[2] many young families. If you widen this street, you will increase the flow of traffic. Such an increase would present[3] a danger for young children who are walking to school or playing in yards.

Isn't there some other way to expedite[4] traffic? For example, why don't you consider routing the traffic around this neighborhood by increasing[5] the lanes on Jefferson Avenue? In some sections of the city, traffic flow is reversed during different[6] times of the day. This street could serve as a main expressway into the city during the morning and out of the[7] city during the afternoon.

Please do not make a decision on this matter without considering the[8] welfare of the residential community. We request a hearing to allow our views to be heard. Yours truly,[9] (180)

4

Dear Miss Arnold:

Thank you for writing to communicate your concerns about the federal policies affecting[1] international trade. I have considered the materials you sent, and I **want** to commend you on the[2] convincing case you presented.

As the representative of your district, I understand and share your concerns.[3] I must weigh these concerns for agricultural development against those affecting other elements[4] of our economy.

I hope that you will continue to **send** your research and advice to me. I can always[5] benefit from the opinions of informed citizens like you. Cordially yours, (114)

want: wish
send: mail, communicate

5

Dear Ms. Brown:

Thank you for your cooperation during our recent inspection of your restaurant. Included[1] with the enclosures in this letter is a report that gives the results of our evaluation. Also, there[2] is a certificate of approval which states that your establishment has passed our inspection and has achieved[3] the highest rating for sanitary conditions.

As our agent, Jim Harrison, may have explained to you, a[4] law was passed during the last session of the state legislature making it mandatory that we conduct an[5] inspection of every public eating establishment at regular intervals. This action is deemed to be[6] essential to preserve the health and safety standards set forth by the state code.

We wish you continued success in[7] your business, and we look forward to visiting with you again. Yours truly, (154)

LESSON

60

1

Dear Sir or Madam:

The zoning commission will meet at 7:30 p.m. on Wednesday, June 8. The purpose[1] of this meeting will be to consider a request for rezoning 13 acres of land near the intersection[2] of State Road 231 and Interstate 40. The owner of the property has requested that the[3] land, which is currently zoned for agricultural use, be rezoned for industrial use.

Representatives[4] of an industrial firm have expressed interest in purchasing part of the land if the zoning change is granted.[5] Representatives of this firm will be present at the meeting to describe the industrial operation[6] that is being planned for this site.

If you wish to present your views about this zoning request, will you please[7] notify our office by Tuesday that you wish to be recognized? After all views have been presented by the[8] public, the board will conduct a general discussion. Because we expect to give this issue a great deal of[9] consideration before making a decision, voting will not take place before the July meeting. Yours truly,[10] (200)

2

Dear Mr. Preston:

This letter is to acknowledge that we received your request for printed materials. The[1] Federal Communications Commission does make various brochures available free of charge to the public.[2] Some examples of the subject matter covered are as follows: a description of the FCC, information[3] about the broadcasting industry, history of electronics, history of communications,[4] etc. We will gladly send you several copies of our publications for use in your junior and[5] senior classes. They will be mailed to your school immediately.

If you would like to have a complete copy of the[6] rules and regulations of the FCC, you may secure it from the Government Printing Office for a[7] small fee. We are delighted to assist in educational projects whenever possible. Please contact us[8] again when our services are needed. Sincerely yours, (170)

3

MEMO TO: County Extension Agents

The Department of Agriculture is planning to conduct studies in[1] four major areas of conservation. Please see the enclosures for detailed descriptions of each study.[2]

In order to make our research effective, we will need to have a large number of farmers participate in[3] these studies; hence, we are asking all county agents to solicit the cooperation of farmers in their[4] areas. We recommend that the agents begin by arranging group meetings and explaining the procedures[5] to the farmers. Because of the nature of these studies, we are anticipating a good response to our request[6] for volunteers.

Once you have enlisted people for this program, our representatives will set up meetings at[7] locations that are convenient for your group. Materials will be distributed at that time.

We would like[8] to have the list of participants by June 4. Your support of this important program is vital to its success.[9] (180)

4

Dear Mrs. Carson:

Thank you for writing to **notify** us of the changes to be made in your social security[1] payments. Beginning with your next monthly payment, your checks will be deposited directly into your bank[2] account.

This direct-deposit method will ensure that your money arrives at the bank safely and on time.[3]

We apologize for the confusion that resulted from your recent change in address. Future correspondence[4] will be mailed to your **residence** at 301 North Elm Street.

In regard to the amount shown on your checks, the monthly[5] payments are always paid in even dollar amounts. Also, the increase in your monthly payments does not go[6] into effect until July 1.

Please let us know if you have any additional difficulties. Very truly[7] yours, (142)

notify: inform, tell
residence: home, address

5

Dear Ms. Hamilton:

Your request for incorporation has been granted. Enclosed is a certificate which[1] has been signed by the Secretary of State. In addition to the articles of incorporation, we are[2] also enclosing copies of the bylaws of your organization. Duplicate copies of these documents[3] have been filed in our office.

Please note that the enclosed certificate was granted under the new law governing[4] not-for-profit organizations. In accordance with the new legislation, our fee for issuing your[5] certificate is less than that which is ordinarily required for profit organizations. Therefore, we have[6] included a refund with this letter.

We appreciate your patience in waiting for this certificate, Ms.[7] Hamilton. Sincerely yours, (144)

IDENTIFICATION INITIALS
FOR UNITED STATES AND TERRITORIES

Alabama (AL) AL	Massachusetts (MA) MA
Alaska (AK) AK	Michigan (MI) MI
Arizona (AZ) AZ	Minnesota (MN) MN
Arkansas (AR) AR	Mississippi (MS) MS
California (CA) CA	Missouri (MO) MO
Colorado (CO) CO	Montana (MT) MT
Connecticut (CT) CT	Nebraska (NE) NE
Delaware (DE) DE	Nevada (NV) NV
District of Columbia (DC) DC	New Hampshire (NH) NH
Florida (FL) FL	New Jersey (NJ) NJ
Georgia (GA) GA	New Mexico (NM) NM
Hawaii (HI) HI	New York (NY) NY
Idaho (ID) ID	North Carolina (NC) NC
Illinois (IL) IL	North Dakota (ND) ND
Indiana (IN) IN	Ohio (OH) OH
Iowa (IA) IA	Oklahoma (OK) OK
Kansas (KS) KS	Oregon (OR) OR
Kentucky (KY) KY	Pennsylvania (PA) PA
Louisiana (LA) LA	Rhode Island (RI) RI
Maine (ME) ME	South Carolina (SC) SC
Maryland (MD) MD	South Dakota (SD) SD

Tennessee (TN) *TN*

Texas (TX) *TX*

Utah (UT) *UT*

Vermont (VT) *VT*

Virginia (VA) *VA*

Washington (WA) *WA*

West Virginia (WV) *WV*

Wisconsin (WI) *WI*

Wyoming (WY) *WY*

Canal Zone (CZ) *CZ*

Guam (GU) *GU*

Puerto Rico (PR) *PR*

Virgin Islands (VI) *VI*

CANADIAN PROVINCES AND TERRITORIES

Alberta (AB) *AB*

British Columbia (BC) *BC*

Labrador (LB) *LB*

Manitoba (MB) *MB*

New Brunswick (NB) *NB*

Newfoundland (NF) *NF*

Northwest Territories (NT) *NT*

Nova Scotia (NS) *NS*

Ontario (ON) *ON*

Prince Edward Island (PE) *PE*

Quebec (PQ) *PQ*

Saskatchewan (SK) *SK*

Yukon Territory (YT) *YT*

AMERICAN CITIES

City	Shorthand
Akron	*acrn*
Albany	*Abne*
Albuquerque	*Abcrce*
Allentown	*Anton*
Atlanta	*alena*
Austin	*asn*
Baltimore	*blt*
Baton Rouge	*btn rz*
Birmingham	*brngh*
Boston	*bsn*
Bridgeport	*brjpl*
Buffalo	*bflo*
Charleston	*Crlsn*
Charlotte	*srll*
Chattanooga	*Clnga*
Chicago	*scg*
Cincinnati	*sNnle*
Cleveland	*clvln*
Colorado Springs	*CO sprgs*
Columbia	*clnba*
Columbus	*clnbs*

City	Shorthand
Dallas	*dls*
Davenport	*dvnpl*
Dayton	*dln*
Denver	*dnvr*
Des Moines	*d yn*
Detroit	*dlryl*
El Paso	*el pso*
Flint	*fln*
Fort Lauderdale	*fl ldrdl*
Fort Worth	*fl rl*
Fresno	*frzno*
Grand Rapids	*grN rpds*
Harrisburg	*hrsbrq*
Hartford	*hrlfd*
Honolulu	*hnllu*
Houston	*hsn*
Indianapolis	*Nenpls*
Jackson	*jcsn*
Jacksonville	*jcsnvl*
Jersey City	*jrze sle*
Kansas City	*KS sle*

Knoxville *nxvl*

Lansing *lNg*

Las Vegas *ls vgs*

Little Rock *lll rc*

Los Angeles *ls ayls*

Louisville *luvl*

Memphis *mfs*

Miami *~ne*

Milwaukee *~lce*

Minneapolis *mepls*

Mobile *~B*

Nashville *nsvl*

New Haven *nu hvn*

New Orleans *nu orlns*

New York *NY*

Newark *nurc*

Newport News *nupt nz*

Norfolk *nrfc*

Oakland *oclN*

Oklahoma City *OK sle*

Omaha *o~ha*

Orlando *orlNo*

Peoria *pera*

Philadelphia *fldlfa*

Phoenix *fnx*

Pittsburgh *plsbrg*

Portland *pllN*

Providence *PvdN*

Richmond *rCmd*

Rochester *rCSr*

Sacramento *scrmlo*

St. Louis *sN lus*

St. Paul *sN pl*

St. Petersburg *sN plsbrg*

Salt Lake City *sll lc sle*

San Antonio *sn alno*

San Bernardino *sn brnrdno*

San Diego *sn deg*

San Francisco *sn frnssco*

San Jose *sn hza*

Sarasota *srsla*

Scranton *scrNn*

Seattle *sell*

Shreveport *srvpl*

Spokane *spcn*

Springfield *sprgfld*

Syracuse *srcs*

Tacoma *tcma*

Tampa *tmpa*

Toledo *tldo*

Trenton *trntn*

Tucson *tsn*

Tulsa *tlsa*

West Palm Beach *Wpm bC*

Wichita *Cla*

Wilmington *wlgtn*

Worcester *Sr*

Youngstown *ygston*

CANADIAN CITIES

Brampton *brmtn*

Burlington *brlgtn*

Burnaby *brnbe*

Calgary *clgre*

East York *E yrc*

Edmonton *edmntn*

Etobicoke *etbcc*

Halifax *hlfx*

Hamilton *hmltn*

Kitchener *ctnr*

Laval *lvl*

London *lntn*

Mississauga *Msga*

Montreal *mtrel*

Oshawa *osa*

Ottawa *ota*

Quebec *qbc*

Regina *rjna*

St. Catharines *sN clrns*

Saskatoon *sscln*

Thunder Bay *tNr ba*

Toronto *trnto*

Vancouver *vncvr*

Windsor *nzr*

Winnipeg *npg*

York *yrc*

READING RATE (words per minute)

Words in Letter	80	90	100	110	120	130	140	150	160	170	180	190	200
82	1:01	0:55	0:49	0:45	0:41	0:38	0:35	0:33	0:31	0:29	0:28	0:26	0:25
84	1:03	0:56	0:50	0:46	0:42	0:39	0:36	0:34	0:31	0:29	0:28	0:27	0:25
86	1:04	0:57	0:52	0:47	0:43	0:40	0:37	0:34	0:32	0:31	0:29	0:27	0:26
88	1:06	0:59	0:53	0:48	0:44	0:41	0:38	0:35	0:33	0:31	0:29	0:28	0:26
90	1:08	1:00	0:54	0:49	0:45	0:42	0:39	0:36	0:34	0:32	0:30	0:28	0:27
92	1:09	1:01	0:55	0:50	0:46	0:42	0:39	0:37	0:34	0:32	0:31	0:29	0:28
94	1:10	1:03	0:56	0:51	0:47	0:43	0:40	0:38	0:35	0:33	0:31	0:30	0:28
96	1:12	1:04	0:58	0:52	0:48	0:44	0:41	0:38	0:36	0:34	0:32	0:30	0:29
98	1:13	1:05	0:59	0:53	0:49	0:45	0:42	0:39	0:37	0:35	0:32	0:31	0:29
100	1:15	1:07	1:00	0:55	0:50	0:46	0:43	0:40	0:38	0:35	0:34	0:32	0:30
102	1:16	1:08	1:01	0:56	0:51	0:47	0:44	0:41	0:38	0:36	0:34	0:32	0:31
104	1:18	1:09	1:02	0:57	0:52	0:48	0:45	0:42	0:39	0:37	0:35	0:33	0:31
106	1:19	1:11	1:04	0:58	0:53	0:49	0:45	0:42	0:40	0:37	0:35	0:33	0:32
108	1:21	1:12	1:05	0:59	0:54	0:50	0:46	0:43	0:40	0:38	0:36	0:34	0:32
110	1:23	1:13	1:06	1:00	0:55	0:51	0:47	0:44	0:41	0:39	0:37	0:35	0:33
112	1:24	1:15	1:07	1:01	0:56	0:52	0:48	0:45	0:42	0:40	0:37	0:35	0:34
114	1:25	1:16	1:08	1:02	0:57	0:53	0:49	0:46	0:43	0:40	0:38	0:36	0:34
116	1:27	1:17	1:10	1:03	0:58	0:54	0:50	0:46	0:43	0:41	0:38	0:37	0:35
118	1:28	1:19	1:11	1:04	0:59	0:54	0:51	0:47	0:44	0:41	0:40	0:37	0:35
120	1:30	1:20	1:12	1:05	1:00	0:55	0:51	0:48	0:45	0:43	0:40	0:38	0:36
122	1:31	1:21	1:13	1:07	1:01	0:56	0:52	0:49	0:46	0:43	0:41	0:39	0:37
124	1:33	1:23	1:14	1:08	1:02	0:57	0:53	0:50	0:46	0:44	0:41	0:39	0:37
126	1:34	1:24	1:16	1:09	1:03	0:58	0:54	0:50	0:47	0:44	0:42	0:40	0:38
128	1:36	1:25	1:17	1:10	1:04	0:59	0:55	0:51	0:48	0:45	0:43	0:40	0:38
130	1:38	1:27	1:18	1:11	1:05	1:00	0:56	0:52	0:49	0:46	0:43	0:41	0:39
132	1:39	1:28	1:19	1:12	1:06	1:01	0:57	0:53	0:49	0:47	0:44	0:42	0:40
134	1:40	1:29	1:20	1:13	1:07	1:02	0:57	0:54	0:50	0:47	0:44	0:42	0:40
136	1:42	1:31	1:22	1:14	1:08	1:03	0:58	0:54	0:51	0:48	0:46	0:43	0:41
138	1:43	1:32	1:23	1:15	1:09	1:04	0:59	0:55	0:52	0:49	0:46	0:44	0:41
140	1:45	1:33	1:24	1:16	1:10	1:05	1:00	0:56	0:53	0:49	0:47	0:44	0:42

Words in Letter	80	90	100	110	120	130	140	150	160	170	180	190	200
142	1:47	1:35	1:25	1:17	1:11	1:06	1:01	0:57	0:53	0:50	0:47	0:45	0:43
144	1:48	1:36	1:26	1:19	1:12	1:06	1:02	0:58	0:54	0:51	0:48	0:45	0:43
146	1:50	1:37	1:28	1:20	1:13	1:07	1:03	0:58	0:55	0:52	0:49	0:46	0:44
148	1:51	1:39	1:29	1:21	1:14	1:08	1:03	0:59	0:56	0:52	0:49	0:47	0:44
150	1:53	1:40	1:30	1:22	1:15	1:09	1:04	1:00	0:56	0:53	0:50	0:47	0:45
152	1:54	1:41	1:31	1:23	1:16	1:10	1:05	1:01	0:57	0:54	0:51	0:48	0:46
154	1:56	1:43	1:32	1:24	1:17	1:11	1:06	1:02	0:58	0:54	0:51	0:49	0:46
156	1:57	1:44	1:34	1:25	1:18	1:12	1:07	1:02	0:59	0:55	0:52	0:49	0:47
158	1:59	1:45	1:35	1:26	1:19	1:13	1:08	1:03	0:59	0:56	0:53	0:50	0:47
160	2:00	1:47	1:36	1:27	1:20	1:14	1:09	1:04	1:00	0:56	0:53	0:51	0:48
162	2:02	1:48	1:37	1:28	1:21	1:15	1:09	1:05	1:01	0:57	0:54	0:51	0:49
164	2:03	1:49	1:38	1:29	1:22	1:16	1:10	1:06	1:02	0:58	0:55	0:52	0:49
166	2:05	1:51	1:40	1:31	1:23	1:17	1:11	1:06	1:02	0:59	0:55	0:52	0:50
168	2:06	1:52	1:41	1:32	1:24	1:18	1:12	1:07	1:03	0:59	0:56	0:53	0:50
170	2:08	1:53	1:42	1:33	1:25	1:18	1:13	1:08	1:04	1:00	0:57	0:54	0:51
172	2:09	1:55	1:43	1:34	1:26	1:19	1:14	1:09	1:05	1:01	0:57	0:54	0:52
174	2:11	1:56	1:44	1:35	1:27	1:20	1:15	1:10	1:05	1:01	0:58	0:55	0:52
176	2:12	1:57	1:46	1:36	1:28	1:21	1:15	1:10	1:06	1:02	0:59	0:56	0:53
178	2:14	1:59	1:47	1:37	1:29	1:22	1:16	1:11	1:07	1:03	0:59	0:56	0:54
180	2:15	2:00	1:48	1:38	1:30	1:23	1:17	1:12	1:08	1:04	1:00	0:57	0:54
182	2:17	2:01	1:49	1:39	1:31	1:24	1:18	1:13	1:08	1:04	1:01	0:57	0:55
184	2:18	2:03	1:50	1:40	1:32	1:25	1:19	1:14	1:09	1:05	1:01	0:58	0:55
186	2:20	2:04	1:52	1:41	1:33	1:26	1:20	1:14	1:10	1:06	1:02	0:59	0:56
188	2:21	2:05	1:53	1:43	1:34	1:27	1:21	1:15	1:11	1:06	1:03	0:59	0:56
190	2:23	2:07	1:54	1:44	1:35	1:28	1:21	1:16	1:11	1:07	1:03	1:00	0:57
192	2:24	2:08	1:55	1:45	1:36	1:29	1:22	1:17	1:12	1:08	1:04	1:01	0:58
194	2:26	2:09	1:56	1:46	1:37	1:30	1:23	1:18	1:13	1:08	1:05	1:01	0:58
196	2:27	2:11	1:58	1:47	1:38	1:30	1:24	1:18	1:14	1:09	1:05	1:02	0:59
198	2:29	2:12	1:59	1:48	1:39	1:31	1:25	1:19	1:14	1:10	1:06	1:03	0:59
200	2:30	2:13	2:00	1:49	1:40	1:32	1:26	1:20	1:15	1:11	1:07	1:03	1:00